If Someone Says "You Complete Me," RUN!

ALSO BY
WHOOPI GOLDBERG

If Someone Says "You Complete Me," RUN!

Whoopi's Big Book of Relationships

WHOOPI GOLDBERG

hachette
BOOKS

NEW YORK   BOSTON

Hachette Books
Hachette Book Group
1290 Avenue of the Americas
New York, NY 10104
HachetteBookGroup.com

Printed in the United States of America

RRD-C

First Edition: October 2015

10 9 8 7 6 5 4 3 2 1

Hachette Books is a division of Hachette Book Group, Inc. The Hachette Books name and logo are trademarks of Hachette Book Group, Inc.

The publisher is not responsible for websites (or their content) that are not owned by the publisher.

Library of Congress Cataloging-in-Publication Data is available upon request.

ISBN 978-0-316-30201-2 (hardcover edition)
ISBN 978-0-316-38778-1 (large print edition)
ISBN 978-0-316-39124-5 (B&N signed edition)

To my entire family, past and present
For all the relationships I had or ever will have
And especially to my brother Clyde

During the time that I was writing this book, my big brother, Clyde, passed away. For me, he was the greatest big brother one could have. When I was little and his friends complained that he was bringing his little sister everywhere, he would say, "Either she comes or I don't go." We remained very close in our early years, and then kind of drifted apart for many reasons in our twenties and thirties. In our late thirties we came back together; he became my driver and my confidant for years. The adventures were many. Somewhat wild. And nothing we can talk about in this book.

As you may know, my family was very small. It was just my mother, my brother, and me. And there's something to be said for the Three Musketeers.

The loss of Clyde was a big surprise, and something that I'm sure won't hit me fully for a long time. I'm dedicating this book to him because what I write about here evolved over a lot of conversations he and I had together on these very subjects.

Contents

Contents

INTRODUCTION

Hey! I'm really glad you picked up this book. People had a lot to say when they heard I was writing this: "How dare you," "Why do you think you can write this?" "You're not a shrink, you're not even a TV Judge." Well, that's all correct. I'm just Whoopi, who has a lot of fun and who has made a few mistakes along the way, and I hope to help you steer clear of the common mistakes we ALL seem to make.

I came to the conclusion that for me the things that are required in a relationship are not things I'm willing to do. Wow! I don't know if I've heard anyone say that out loud or if I've read it in a book anywhere else.

What I hope, though, is that you read this and say, "Hey, I'm going to try that, it makes perfect sense," or "Maybe not" and then you can move on to the next chapter. I can't be everything to everyone all the time, so some of this may not work for you. These are just suggestions.

You can read this book in the bathroom; no one will

have to know. You can quote it on occasion to other people who are making the same sort of jumps or "mistakes" that you've already made.

The point is, this is what I figured out for me. If it works for you, great, and if it doesn't, there is always another book for you somewhere else.

So, read on, and I hope for you the very best.

Whoopi Goldberg
NYC 2015

If Someone Says
"You Complete Me,"
RUN!

CHAPTER ONE

Leave It to Beavers

For the past seven or eight years, I've have been sitting on *The View*, a supposed women's talk show that deals with what women want. I have to say I've been kind of surprised by a lot of women's responses to things said on the show. And I thought this was odd, because I *am* a woman, right? Still, a lot of the things I have heard—and still hear—on the show regarding relationships just don't make a lot of sense to me. And if what I am hearing from other women about what they want makes no sense to me, there is clearly a disconnect. So I feel I have to address this.

Before we get into the nitty-gritty, let's start at the

very beginning. That's always a very good place to
start.

We've all been brainwashed with false expectations.

That's right. Brainwashed.

For example, when you're watching the Nature chan-
nel and see animals that have mated—lions, let's say. So
with lions, you know there's the pride, which is the lions'
big extended family or pack: the big mammy lion and the
papa lion and the baby lions, and they are all together,
right? They don't futz around, I don't think. The mammy
lion goes out and gets the gazelle and brings it back, and
she eats first and then she leaves the rest for the papa
lion—or the other way around. But the point is, they are
one big happy family.

And penguins. You know how cute they are. The
mother penguin walks across the tundra to lay the egg,
and the father comes and sits on the egg, and the mother
goes and swims, just like in *Happy Feet*. Then the mother
comes back up with a draggle of food to feed everybody.
And they're all one big happy family.

You look at the monkeys. Monkeys mate for life. And
whales. And wolves. Plenty of animals mate for life: Gib-
bons and titi monkeys. Swans. Black vultures. French
angel fish (but not American angel fish, which seems
backward, given the French's tendency for mistresses...).
The albatross. Termites. Bald eagles. Barn owls. Bats. Prai-

rie voles (which look like little rats). Turtle doves. *Schistosoma mansoni* worms.

My point is that from the time you're a little kid, you're getting all these signals of what love and marriage and family are supposed to be. Some people even bring religion into it and say that's the way God intended it. That two people are supposed to be together forever.

But not every species mates for life.

Dolphins do not mate for life. They do, however, have the ability to create strong, long-lasting relationships with one another, and some species of dolphin may even travel with several generations of family members. For instance, the killer whale—actually a dolphin, by the way—may be found swimming with up to three generations of family members within its pod. However, these dolphins will mate only with partners outside their pod, in order to prevent intercourse with other family members—what we humans would call incest. In fact, most species of dolphins are very sexual animals and are known to mate with several partners throughout the course of a year. Some dolphin species may even choose to have sex at any time of the year, unlike some of the whale species, which hook up only during their mating season. Not all dolphin species mate equally during the course of the year, though.

Yet, given the mythology of relationships I'd been exposed to, I thought dolphins mated for life. Until I did my research and learned that, in fact, most species *do not* mate for life.

What you may have noticed missing in these descriptions of animals that mate for life, and what the research makes clear, is that nowhere on this list is Man.

And nowhere on this list is Woman.

We, I think, are the only species that can choose when to have sex or whom to have sex with. We're not like other animals, who are doing it to procreate and get stuff done.

Except the apes—they love to fuck. They just do. I don't know why. Chimps and bonobos, in particular. They will bone everybody and anybody. Apes just happen to be our closest relatives in the animal kingdom, which isn't to say we will bone just about anybody and everybody. Although some of us will…

Anyway, as we look at these lists of who mates for life, we see that humans are nowhere to be found. I think that's a big deal. Maybe if we knew that when we got together with someone or got married, that it didn't have to be for life, perhaps we would be better at it.

When I was growing up, there was this whole *Leave It to Beaver* ideal we were all supposed to live up to. I grew up in a housing project in Chelsea, New York, and there were all sorts of people there—blacks, whites, Asians, yellow people, brown people, orange people, gays, straights, big people, little people, you name it (if

I've left out your ethnic group, shoe size, or orientation, just insert it here)—all living together.

And single working mothers were the norm. My mother raised my brother, Clyde, and me on her own while going to work every day. She was elegant and smart, but she wasn't Donna Reed.

Wait, do you even know who Donna Reed is? No? How about Carol Brady?

Anyway, my mother was better than these idealized moms. She was tougher and stronger and stricter, and it took just one look at her to know she was no-nonsense.

And if my mother wasn't Carol Brady, my elder brother, Clyde, was no freckle-faced Beaver Cleaver...or Bobby Brady. If we each have a personal soundtrack following us around in life, Clyde's would have been the theme song from *Shaft*. He was *that* cool.

My mother and my brother gave me everything: they loved me and supported me and gave me the confidence I needed to go out in the world and do what I do. I felt like we were normal. But for some reason, in today's world, the kind of family I had isn't considered normal.

This idea of being "normal" and having a so-called "normal" family doesn't really ring true for a whole lot of folks. If for anyone. Yet we are told that's what we are supposed to strive for.

Meeting someone and staying with them forever, or

however long you live, has been ingrained in all of us somehow, and yet, up until the last century, who lived past forty? They didn't have time for more than one or two spouses. They had no choice but to stay together, because they were dead before they knew it...

Okay, maybe that's too harsh, but you get my drift.

Today we live much longer, and therefore have more time to screw things up, and we do. We oftentimes set ourselves up to fail, men and women. No one is spared... except...sometimes...maybe we give men a pass when they screw up because we figure they can't help themselves and just want to plug a hole—even though we know there is more to them than that.

As a grown-up, I kind of feel you have to look at a person as a person. Each person is their own special individual.

Awwwww.

There's nobody more complicated than a human being. Straight, gay, black, white, or "other"—it doesn't matter. The position we put ourselves in is incredibly complicated—mostly because we complicate it. My search in the last several years has been for how to be in an uncomplicated situation (aka relationship).

As you read this book, know that these are *my* solutions. They're what I learned for *me*. I'm sharing them with you 'cause I would have liked someone to say to me a long time ago, "Hey, think about this!" This is what I would like to have said to myself, if I could have written a letter to my younger self.

Along with, "Keep the bra."

What I learned is I have to be honest about what I want.

For most of us, when we were little, we had this sweet idea—whether you're a guy or a girl—that we would have this fairy-tale relationship, and the little birds would fly up to us and eat from our hands, and we would walk off into the sunset, and it would be brilliant and fantastic, and we would be perfect for each other.

But it usually doesn't work like that, does it?

CHAPTER TWO

I Want to Know What Love Is

Spoiler alert: This chapter doesn't have any real advice. I just go on a rant about where these crazy ideas about relationships come from. So stick with me.

When you think about all the cultural factors that influence you in terms of setting expectations for the kinds of relationships you look for, it can blow your mind. I grew up in the sixties and can pinpoint, specifically, the impact the Beatles had on me. When you listen to "She Loves You," or any of their songs, you just want to...well, let's put it this way: *that's* what you want. You want *that* kind of relationship. "And I Love Her" is also one that just gets you. It's crazy. And "Love Me Do." I could go on and on. All those songs lead you to believe that this is what's out there waiting for you. That if you're careful and you're smart and you're loving, you're going to find it.

When you listen to any of Sinatra's songs, it's kind of extraordinary how deeply affecting they are. Fundamentally, Ol' Blue Eyes was singing about great relationships or about stumbling upon someone amazing, like in "Strangers in the Night." It's what you basically want.

Then you end up with somebody like Barry White, and it's all about sex. It's just too much; it's overkill. You're just like, "Come on. Are you kidding me?"

In the fifties and sixties, it was all about the romance. All these songs that make us feel such strong emotions also make us think, "Wouldn't it be great if life were like that?" Think about any of the Four Seasons songs. You want to be their Ronnie. You want to be that girl.

But our lives are much harder and more complicated than a three-minute song.

All these romantic songs created a bunch of hopeless romantics—no wonder the seventies turned into the decade of divorce. The women's movement and the Pill helped all this along. Real life couldn't compete with what we were listening to. When you realize that your idea of perfect love was shaped by the music you listened to, things start to get a lot clearer and make much more sense.

This may say a lot about why people are the way they are these days about love. Songs like "It's Hard Out Here for a Pimp" might have deeply shifted our concept of love...I'm kidding.

The Beatles weren't the only ones. Think about all these songs that you hear today that help heighten this idea of what a relationship should be.

John Legend has a song called "Good Morning." Even I, when I hear it, think for one hot second, "Wouldn't it be nice to have somebody sing that to me or feel that way about me?" The words are "Good morning, good morning, love." It's just, like, "Well, good morning, John." Who the hell doesn't want to wake up to John Legend singing to them about how wonderful they are? It's not a bad way to start the day.

Or listen to "(You Make Me Feel Like) A Natural Woman." Really? There's someone out there who is going to make you feel like a "natural woman," as if you were an "unnatural woman" to start with? Or "As Long as He Needs Me," from the musical *Oliver!*, where Nancy sings about Bill Sykes, who has pretty much beat the shit out of her, and she is saying, "This is my man, and I'm going to be with him even though he doesn't do any of the things that he is supposed to do, just because I think that, deep down, he needs me." What the hell is wrong with this woman?

Think about "I Say a Little Prayer": "The moment I wake up / Before I put on my makeup, / I say a little prayer for you." Come on. Really? What the fuck? You should be saying a little prayer for yourself, so you can get through the day. If you're going to take a minute to pray, pray that you get to your job on time without getting hit by a bus or getting mugged, or that nothing happens to you on the subway or crossing the street. This idea that you have this love, this love in you, and you say a little prayer for *him* every morning before you do anything else…it's not really real. It's kind of wonderful to be in that heightened state, but it's not real. Maybe I just look at it as a prelude to problems, because at some point you won't be so infatuated or giddy or oversexed, and you will be sorely disappointed. Which is when you start saying a little prayer that this person will just go away.

For me, these are the worst songs to listen to if you are looking for love. I blame these songs for messing me up, for setting me up to fail. Don't get me wrong. They are all great songs. I love these songs. They just send the wrong message:

■ "I Want to Know What Love Is," by Foreigner. Boy does this one suck people in. I love the title—and who *doesn't* want to know what love is? But then here is the trap: "I know you can show me." Come on. It's a trap.

■ "What a Difference a Day Makes," by Dinah Washington. So she meets this guy, and in twenty-four hours her whole life turns around from misery to bliss? I can only say, "Good luck, sistah."

■ "My Boy Lollipop." Let's not even get into why she is calling her boyfriend a lollipop. You know what I'm talking about.

■ "It's a Man's Man's Man's World," and pretty much James Brown all around. As the saying goes, women today have half the money and all the pussy, so I'm not sure this song is accurate.

■ "I Can't Make You Love Me." This song is a real heartbreaker, and Bonnie Raitt just kills it. This song will make you cry, but it could also send you into a tailspin of heartbreak that just isn't right.

■ "Where Would I Be Without You?" by the Supremes. Hopefully still yourself.

■ A lot of Stevie Wonder, especially "I Believe (When I Fall in Love, It Will Be Forever)." The whole album that this song is on, *Talking Book*, pretty much covers the entire trajectory of a relationship. It is amazing, but you are going to want to break out the scotch when you listen to that one.

■ Any of the love songs from *West Side Story*, but especially "One Hand, One Heart." So now we all want to be Siamese twins?

■ "My Girl." Providing sunshine on a cloudy day and some of these other acts of God the Temptations sing about is a lot of pressure to put on someone. Do you really want to take that on and be that guy's girl?

When I hear songs like this I'm thinking, "This is why we have no idea how to behave with each other in a relationship! Because there's all this mythology about what a relationship should be." And it is a far cry from reality.

All these songs send the wrong message. They make you weak and want to wallow, and love isn't about being weak and wallowing. We all have those songs that we love to wallow in or use to beat ourselves up when we're down. It's a bittersweet kind of thing we do to ourselves.

Let's do a little exercise. What are five to ten songs that you love and use to set up unrealistic expectations for yourself or your relationship? Or those that have set you up to fail? Really think about it, and list them here:

1) _____

2) _____

3) _____

4) _____

5) _____

6) _____

7) _____

8) _____

9) _____

10) _____

Now let's look at movies, television, and even commercials.

I am a huge movie buff, but that shit can mess you up. In a way, popular culture conditions us to find someone who makes us happy which many of us take to mean "Just find someone, whether they make you happy or not. Just find someone or you won't be considered normal." That's why so many people rush into relationships that make no sense.

Women in particular are told you've got to find somebody because your biological clock is ticking. Well, if the only reason you're looking for somebody is because your clock is ticking, just have a baby on your own, because I always say if you mate to make a baby, everything else goes by the wayside. After a baby, you and a boyfriend may end up hating each other, loving each other, or just tolerating each other. It doesn't matter. You're going to love the baby, and Baby comes first. If you really want a child you just might be better off having one on your own rather than dragging the wrong person into it.

(As a side note to all my Christian friends, whose heads may be exploding right now: I am not antimarriage, and I am not anti-two-parent homes. Take what I am saying as an exploration of "There's got to be a better way." So you don't need to tweet me, call me, write me letters. You don't have to do that.)

This idea to find somebody and couple up also makes people who are not interested in coupling up, or who at this point in their lives are not coupled up, feel terrible. It makes us ask ourselves, "Is there something wrong with me? Why doesn't someone want me?"

Which brings me back to movies: Remember Bridget Jones at that dinner party where she is the only "singleton," as Bridget would say—you know she and I are tight—and everyone else is a "smug married"? Why should she have to feel bad? The smug marrieds at that party are acting like assholes. Why should she be single shamed? She wants a relationship; she is trying. She is also a flawed human being who knows how hard these things can be and who still has the guts to keep trying.

No one should feel like they have to have someone there with them to show outside people that they're worthy. It takes a solid person who knows who she is to go to the dinner party by herself and hold her own.

Women in this country feel that they in particular have been kind of set up. 'Cause they think a romantic relationship and marriage are the be-all and end-all, and the things they are supposed to be striving for—myself included. I tried to get that brass ring. Three times! And it choked me. I thought that in order to be "normal," I had to be married. So I got married even though I knew it wasn't right. When that didn't work out I tried it again. And then again.

We push people in a desperate fashion to find someone, because everything we see, feel, and read oftentimes is about someone finding that perfect person. So you're looking and looking. You see somebody who looks halfway decent, and out of desperation you decide he or she is the one—as if there is only "one" out there for each of us (which is a whole other subject). We decide that this halfway-decent person is "the one" and try to make the square peg fit into the round hole, which always ends badly.

Now, don't get me wrong, there are a lot of great couples out there who found a way to do it, to make it last a lifetime, you know, and God bless them. Like Anne and Eli Wallach, Jerry Stiller and Anne Meara, Sidney Poitier and Joanna. Paul Newman and Joanne Woodward. Ronald and Nancy Reagan. The Bush families. Bill and Hillary Clinton. It can happen. It can work, but you don't know the compromises each of these people had to make in order to stay together. To them, it was clearly important to accept those compromises to maintain the relationship, because it was their priority.

I know lots of people who stayed together as long as they could. Susan Sarandon and Tim Robbins, for example. They never got married, but it lasted as long as it was supposed to last.

But let's go back to the origins of these fantasies we have. Where do they all come from? Music is a part of it, yes. But, again, think about the mythology of movies.

Of course, all this is coming from someone who once

facilitated a tearjerker of a reunion from the beyond between a woman and her dead husband in one of the most hopelessly romantic movies of all time! (And believe me, I am eternally grateful for that role, but I'm just saying…)

An Officer and a Gentleman. Pretty Woman. Fifty Shades of Grey. (They call the last one Mommy Porn, but really, it wasn't about the sex; it was about the money, at least in the book. Not that many people want to be flagellated, you know, whipped, for those of you who haven't seen it—which isn't to knock it for those people who do.) *Footloose. The Enchanted Cottage. Grease. Twilight. Can't Buy Me Love. The Notebook.* (Or any fucking book or movie by Nicholas Sparks.) Then there's Rhett Butler and Scarlett O'Hara in *Gone With the Wind.* Maria and Tony in *West Side Story.* Really? You're going to die for love after knowing each other for less than twenty-four hours? I love that movie, but come on!

"But its true love!" some will say.

But it ain't real, people. It's a movie.

These are wonderful fantasies about love that rises above and beyond the normal human condition. And we have been programmed to think that this is what relationships are supposed to look like. We think these movies give us hope, but in reality they just create false expectations that will come back and bite us in the butt.

What extremely successful, gorgeous man is going to

pick up a lady of the evening off the street? Honestly? Billionaires tend to go for the high-class escorts or call girls. He might possibly buy her a designer dress, fall in love with her, and marry her. (I'm not naming names here.) Think about it, though: if someone who looked like Julia Roberts were working the streets, TMZ would be all over it.

Everybody wants that kind of magic thing that happens in romantic movies. Everyone wants to think that love can conquer all and overcome any problem, but it doesn't always work that way in real life.

Some of the absolute worst movies when it comes to setting people up are also some of the most popular. They are ridiculously romantic, but they aren't realistic. Do not watch these if you are looking for love. They might be really wonderful movies, but they tend to lead you astray.

1. *Fifty Shades of Grey.* The absolute worst.

2. *Jerry Maguire.* The title of this book comes from the most famous line in this movie.

3. Almost anything with the younger Julia Roberts in it, but without question *Pretty Woman.*

4. *The Notebook* and any other movie based on a book by Nicholas Sparks.

5. Any movie that makes you cry uncontrollably for no reason, or makes you look at your partner and wish he would be replaced by the leading man.

Now give me the five to ten that have led you the most astray:

1) _____

2) _____

3) _____

4) _____

5) _____

6)-10) _____

Never watch those movies again. Delete them from your watch list and replace them with something more relevant to real life or at the very least know that they are nothing but fantasy escapism, like *Game of Thrones*. You can get pleasure from the escapism, but don't mistake it for real life.

While some of us may think we have a soundtrack to our life, none of us gets our own movie soundtrack. This means that we may have songs that have been important to us at times in our life, our history, but none of us has an actual soundtrack playing in the background.

In *Manhattan*, with Woody Allen and Diane Keaton, you hear Gershwin in the background while they are walking down the street. That's not happening in real life. No one hears fucking Gershwin when they are out walking. You hear, "Honk, honk, move!" You see dogs pooping. You hear people talking loudly on their cell phones. You're exposed to all that. In the movies, none of that.

That should tell you to be really careful in how movies relate to your real life. If you're attracted to what you see in the movies, and you're looking for that, the first thing you need to know is that it's not real. The way you know it's not real is that no one in the movie steps in dog shit. Chances are that movie relationship is not real, either.

We all go through it; it's how we're conditioned.

I have a friend who was watching *Twilight*, and her

husband was sleeping on the couch next to her. And that damn vampire got to her.

She thought to herself, "Why didn't I fucking marry a vampire? Here I am stuck with you, and all I want is the vampire."

When she told me this, I said to her, "Really? Do you really want to be married to a vampire who sucks your blood, is dead and deadly, and may eventually kill you? I don't think so."

The craziest stuff you can think of has been conditioned in us.

And by the way, can anyone explain how vampires, who have no blood in them, get an erection?...Just asking.

I was watching a terrific old movie, *Stella Dallas*, not long ago. You have the good woman, and she's married to the rich guy, but the rich guy likes the girl from the other side of the tracks. They have an affair, and then she has his baby, and then the man comes to her and says, "I want the baby. My wife and I are going to raise the baby to be ours, and we will give it everything you can't give it." She goes, "No, don't take my baby." But then her maternal instincts kick in and she thinks, "Maybe he is right," so she gives them the kid.

Several years later, the baby girl is all grown up and going to get married, and the real mom happens to be walking by the brownstone where the wedding is taking place. She stands outside, this fallen woman, and she watches her daughter get married from afar.

And I'm thinking, "What the fuck? Go in and tell her that you're there!" It was driving me crazy. Never mind that today this would have ended up in court with a paternity suit, custody battle, and child support. But this movie was driving me crazy because what you realize after a certain age, and after a certain amount of time being around people, is that people around you play out scenarios they've seen in the movies. And you realize, "Oh, my God, what we see is in us."

That shit is just in us.

This bullshit even comes from commercials. You see the couple, they are taking a bath together, looking out at the sunset, with giant grins on their faces because he is using Viagra. I don't know very many couples who sit in a bathtub watching a sunset, but maybe I don't travel in the correct kind of circles.

What I'd like to know is what are they talking about? Is she saying the stuff that comes in the middle of a relationship, like "Why don't you ever put the fucking toilet seat down?" "Why don't you put the cap on the toothpaste?" "Why do you leave dishes in the sink?"

No, she is happy and smiling because this is a commercial written by men for men, and the woman is supposed to be smiling because her guy is going to have a hard-on for the next four hours. So who cares whether he replaced that toilet paper roll?

My biggest problem has always been that I love the idea of being in love and all the things that it suggests. Walking hand in hand, instinctually knowing what the other person wants, and looking up and seeing your love looking at you in that special soft-focus way people look at each other in the movies. We all want somebody who will fight for our love. In real life, we actually have to put the effort out. But because we are in love with the idea of being in love, we keep getting married or hooking up because we think, "I must be doing something wrong. Let's try this again with somebody else," as opposed to, "Hey! Maybe what I'm looking for isn't real. It doesn't exist. It's a fantasy." It isn't like we are all looking for a knight in shining armor necessarily, but we are looking for someone who makes us feel like the leading man or the leading lady in a movie.

Beyond the pop culture mythology that sets us up for disappointment when it comes to love, the reality is that relationships are really hard and we can all get on each other's nerves from time to time. We spend half our lives trying to find a relationship, and then, when we finally get one and all of it is right there in front of us, the good, the bad, and the very ugly, it becomes about

"Jesus Christ, can you make the bed every once in a while?" Simple dumb stuff.

It's the little stuff that drives you crazy. You wake up one day and realize, "Wow, this is it. Oh, man. I'm going to be sleeping next to you for a long time. I'm going to listen to you gnash your teeth. I'm going to watch you not clean your hair out of the sink. I'm going to watch you smile in your sleep. I'm going to watch you thrash about and steal the covers. I'm going to listen to you fart. I'm going to watch you lie to your boss when you don't want to go to work. I'm just going to have to figure out how to do this for eternity. Etern-a-fucking-ty."

Once we realize that what we see in the movies and what we experience in real life are two separate things, we can learn to change the way we look at things. Most people think that they will find "the one"—that certain special person who makes everything in your life all right. They want to believe love is magic.

While I never thought love was magic, I did think it was going to be very, very different from how it is.

CHAPTER THREE

You Ain't Cinderella

I could write a whole book on "Cinderella." It is a wonderful fairy tale...until you grow up and realize that's really what it is. A fairy tale. It's kind of a wonderful story about a guy who shows up and makes everything all right for a girl and saves her. And they live happily ever after.

If I had to write the sequel to "Cinderella," the first thing she would say in the opening scene is "If you think I'm cleaning this fucking castle, you're out of your mind."

If I'm going to look at "Cinderella," I would say it has evolved into today's British monarchy. In some ways, I'm sure people look at Prince William and Kate and think, "That's the Cinderella story, right?" She was just a commoner, and they got married. They had a couple of kids—a boy and a girl.

As I understand it, though, their story was a bit different from that. It was really kind of fun, because they were in a group of friends, which is apparently how folks tend to find each other now—they just go out in packs. While they were in college, William and Kate were part of the same pack. For a little while they dated, and then they split up. Then he went with this one and that one, and this one and that one. But when he was ready, the one he wanted was Kate. He went back to get her because she had something that really worked for him, and vice versa, I'm sure. That's kind of wonderful. God knows I can't see the future, but I don't feel them divorcing.

When you look at Prince Charles and Camilla, you see that that relationship is a long and strong one, too. It has been going on for years and years. Maybe lifelong. I don't know if they were boning each other before he married Diana, but they knew each other, and there was definitely something going on between them. She's already married with children of her own; Charles has got to get married to somebody else, because he needs an heir. Now, he doesn't mention anything about Camilla to the new one, Diana—he didn't say, "I feel like I have to marry you because this is about the continuation of the monarchy. But I really do love someone else." Although, maybe he should have. That at least would have given Diana a shot at choosing whether to marry him.

Having never been in the monarchy, I believe theirs was a planned kind of marriage. Wasn't there a little pool of women that he could marry? That's the worst beginning and ending. There was no love to begin with, see? There was only the sex, and the sex was for a reason: to create an heir to the throne. I'm sure he liked her, but I think she loved him. Or maybe she thought she did. Or she thought she was supposed to. Who can say? Regardless, the real Cinderella story is Camilla and Charles.

"Cinderella" has done more than almost anything else to give us a false sense of security when it comes to what a marriage or relationship should be. Cinderella, Sleeping Beauty, the Little Mermaid—they all get the guy. That guy just happens to be perfect, and of course they live happily ever after.

Well, I hate to tell it to you, ladies, but that Prince Charming is just a cartoon, not a flesh-and-blood man. And I promise you, you do not want to go to bed every night next to a cartoon.

We drank the Kool-Aid, and the Kool-Aid about what relationships should be like keeps getting poured.

They should be perfect. There should be music. There should be a hunky prince on a white horse sweeping us up and saving us.

None of those things show you the day-to-day work

29

that has to go into a relationship. Whether you're watching the movies that I just talked about or you're watching *My Big Fat Greek Wedding* or *The Donna Reed Show*. My point is, you ain't Cinderella.

Now, I know that, if you're a woman, you can't help but believe in this fantasy. It's in you like blood is in you. You've been conditioned by years and years of happy endings, and not the kind of happy endings you get at a massage parlor. I'm talking about "riding off into the sunset with Prince Charming, on a white horse" happy endings, because that's what movies tell you is going to happen.

On top of that, when you're downtrodden, you get a fairy godmother. Right? When was the last time anybody showed up with a wand and did magic tricks for you? It hasn't happened yet and it never will, unless it happened while you were on LSD in the sixties.

You also don't have no little birds dressing you. You don't have fat little mice turning into stallions to take you to some ball. You don't have any of that.

You might have grown up with a wicked stepmother, that's true. If that was you, then you have one out of the fifty things necessary to actually be Cinderella.

Everywhere you turn, people have romanticized what love is going to be like. And you're like, "I'm going to get married. I'm going to have a big wedding. We're going to do this. We're going to do that. He is going to make it all better for me. He will take out the trash. He will learn how to put stuff up. He will protect me."

I'll just put it to you this way: Girl, you'd better know how to do things for yourself. You'd better learn how to protect yourself, and don't start fights you can't finish. If you want something hung up on the wall, learn how to handle a hammer. You don't want to wait for somebody to do it for you. That's not why you want a relationship. If you want somebody to do stuff for you, get a handyman. It's cheaper, especially if you're going to divorce him. Handymen don't want to get in the bed. He'll just pee in the bathroom, that's all, and hopefully in the toilet and not the sink, like some men I have known. The only problem you'll have with him is he won't put the toilet seat down. But what man does?

My point is when you are looking for a partner, having someone in your life because they can do stuff for you, or because they will take care of you financially, is not a good enough reason. All the things on your checklist of what you want him to be—you'd better equal them.

My question to you: Are you bringing it the way you want him to bring it?

Look in the mirror and ask yourself: Are you the woman Prince Charming is waiting for? Do you have all those attributes? If you're looking for him to be Prince Charming, know that he is looking for you to be Cinderella. (Or Kim Kardashian.) Everybody has that idea. Think about what that means. After marrying Prince Charming, Cinderella moved into the beautiful castle and became the queen. She didn't have a job she had to go to every day, and she didn't have to cook or clean or watch after the children, because she had people to do that for her. She sat around, as most queens do, and waved to people.

In real life, though, somebody has to clean the palace, pay the mortgage, and buy the groceries. Somebody's got to make sure the kids are where they're supposed to be.

So forget it—unless you are willing to adhere to those 1950s fantasies that men seem to still have about the perfect woman. Or, worse yet, that 1970s perfect woman in the perfume commercial who brings home the bacon, fries it up, and never lets him forget he's a man—which I take to mean having sex with him on demand no matter how tired you are. Nineteen fifties or 1970s, they both sound like a raw deal to me, so you just might want to look for the right person who will share all these things with you, and not this so-called Prince Charming.

For you gay women, transpose whatever visual you need to understand what I've written. If yours is a "Princesa Charmita," fine. Either way, I'm talking to you, too, lesbians. If you're waiting for that woman to come along who is going to take care of everything and make you a princess or a queen or whatever—it ain't going to happen.

It. Is. Not. Happening.

So get your heads out of your butts, and stop assuming that everything that's done is done for you or to you or because of you. Take responsibility for yourself, and don't expect someone else to do it for you.

CHAPTER FOUR

You Ain't No Prince Charming

M en: quit looking for your mother. Learn to do stuff on your own. Go to work, and when you come home, help your wife (or husband) with the kids and running the household. Listen to her and appreciate all she does. Don't just pick up the remote and ignore her.

And sometimes size *does* matter.

Explain What the Word *Love* Truly Means

I have to say it's really subjective. What love means to you may not mean the same to me. To me, love is about respect and humor and light. Being light, and being light around people. Now, that may not be what it means to you. It may mean being Cinderella, and a guy comes and sweeps you off your feet. Your ideal may be sharing lots of things, conversations, a love of art or music or culture—love of things that make your lives better. Love may mean a deep emotional connection or a spiritual connection to someone. You have to decide what love is for you, and figure out if you've ever felt it or think you've felt it…or maybe you haven't.

I felt it once. I was in love once, and it was fantastic. He wasn't in the same business as me, and he ended up dying of AIDS, which is one of the most painful things I ever experienced. So at this point in my life,

36

I say I won't ever do it again. It's very tedious and it requires a lot of being there for the other person. That's what it meant then, but when you really love someone, that is what you do. Sometimes it seems like an irrational thing and you will do things you wouldn't do for anyone else.

Yes, I've had a lot of wonderful relationships, but as I've gotten older I've decided I don't want that anymore. At different stages of your life, love can mean different things; it can take many different forms. I have my daughter, my grandchildren, and my great-granddaughter. These are my main connections, my main loves. What it also means? One cat, and my house, which smells like a house without someone else in it.

Why Get into a Relationship?

I don't know. At the start, they are a lot of
fun, there is a lot of excitement and hope
and getting to know one another. There is,
of course, the companionship, having someone to do things with, the conversation,
the connection. But you need to go into
it without expectations, without planning
your entire future after the second date. The
whole process is really about making a new
friend, and then deciding whether you like
that friend enough to do the work that a relationship eventually requires.

As I said in the previous answer, I'm not
keen on relationships myself these days,
because they require a lot of work that I actually don't want to do. If you feel that you
want a partner, and you want to go through
life with someone else who can balance you,
or argue with you, or cry with you, or laugh
with you, and you want it to be more than

your cat, then you're probably ripe for a
relationship.

If you're not willing to do the work, which
requires a bridge, requires you to give and
for the other person to give to you, if you're
not willing to hear why he's upset, if you're
not willing to hear all the things that you
need to hear in a relationship, then maybe
it's not for you.

That's why I'm not in one—because I'm
really someone who needs to figure out
what the cat wants. I spend a lot of time in
the cat box.

CHAPTER FIVE

The Minute You Hear "You Complete Me," Run!

E ver since that movie *Jerry Maguire* came out, with that line where Tom Cruise tells Renée Zellweger, "You complete me," people have wanted to believe in the mushiness of "you complete me" without realizing how bad a situation that is. It may be fantastic screenwriting—it's a great line—but in real life, it's a disaster. If they complete you, they can deconstruct you as well.

Are you a fully realized person? Well, who can say?

Only you know if that's true. But no one you meet is going to make you complete, a fully realized person. You have to be one before you start any of this relationship shit. Otherwise, you're like a goiter attached to somebody, at the whim of how they are feeling. "You complete me." That's such a weird phrase to me. It's almost like you don't have sense enough to do shit on your own. "You complete me." Like, I go to bed, and I'm leaking somewhere because the valve that you are is not there? These visuals are just bullshittian things, and maybe that's part of the problem.

People keep looking for someone to complete them, but that's work you have to do yourself. No one else can do it for you, and if your work isn't complete before you get married or get into a relationship, the relationship will seem a bit shaky, like you're kind of a ghost, a phantom. It's like you're not really there. For someone else to come and work on you as though you were an unfinished painting doesn't seem right. You have to be a complete person before you can commit to anyone else. And the idea that we are walking around as a half person, I find bizarre. Well, think about it. Who are you? Do you have the things you want in your life? Are you okay being alone for a time? Do you have the patience for it?

If you're a complete, whole person, you have the patience to wait for the right person instead of living with someone who isn't for you. Do you have the confidence and faith to wait?

You know when the right one comes along, because you say, "Oh, I could walk with this person side by side, because I know who I am. I know what I like and what I don't want. I know what I will take in my life and what I won't take in my life. This person seems to have a similar feeling. He knows what he likes. He knows who he is." When you come together you're not clashing and fighting and saying, "You're not giving me what I need." You know what you need and you can tell that to the other person. And the other person can say, "I can do that" or "I can't do that."

But you have to recognize when someone is giving you a line of bullshit. You know bullshit when you hear it—that flag goes right up and says, "You know this is a lie, right?" You, as a complete person, know what you are comfortable with, what you can live with, and what you can't. You are not afraid to say, "This is how I feel," or "I don't want someone who is not committed to me," or "I don't want someone who is feeding me bullshit." A complete person is willing to wait to find someone who is committed to her before she commits.

Now let's talk a little more truth.

Do you have the patience for this? Because it could take a long time. Not that there's anything wrong with you, but the right person does not just come floating by in a barrel. You have to open yourself up, pick your tits up, put your eyes up, and hold your head up, because you never know who is out there. If you're walking around looking for perfection in the physical or perfection in the brain or your ideal, because you loved Cinderella or you loved GI Joe, and that's your visual of what your perfect person is, you might want to put that to the side and patiently wait for the person who fulfills your need for truth, justice, and the American Way.

Patient or not, there is no person who completes you. A relationship is a mutual thing and it's about expectations. You may find a person who is willing to try to fulfill what you need, and vice versa. My question to you is can you meet your own expectations? Are you who you want to be? The person who is willing to try to fulfill what you need or don't need? If that doesn't make sense to you, toss this book away and go find a comic book.

So I say if you think getting married is the be-all and end-all of your life, then you really need to think about why you feel that way.

If you're going to do this and get married, really understand yourself and what it is you think it's going to do for you.

If you're doing this because you're lonely, don't do it.

If you're doing this to prove a point, don't do it.

If you're doing this to get back at somebody, don't do it.

If you're doing this because your mother wants you to, don't do it.

If you're doing this because you figure, "What the hell," definitely don't do it.

It takes some strength and energy to go against all the cultural expectations, but it takes even more to live a lie, to get divorced, to fight with someone every day, to be confused or unhappy or untrue to yourself.

So this is a take on the age-old Freudian question "What do women want?" And, of course, to the question all women want an answer to: "What do men want?"

I am saying forget those questions and figure out what *you* want.

I don't know what men want. I don't know what women want. I only know what *I* want. Can you say the same?

At this point, I know what I want and don't want, but it took me a lifetime to figure it out.

This is what I *don't* want:

- To have to think about someone else when I'm feeling selfish.

- To constantly be on the verge of hurting someone else's feelings.

- To be questioned about flushing the toilet.

Ask yourself what you are looking for in a relationship. Maybe that's the question.

Are you looking for someone beautiful?

Are you looking for someone who has a good heart?
A good soul?

Someone you can talk to, someone whose company
you enjoy, someone who is smart, funny?

Maybe you have a vague idea but have never really
spent time thinking about it. You have to walk yourself
through that. Sometimes it changes at different points
in your life, so it's important to check in with yourself
every once in a while.

I can tell you the things that I want in a relationship.
My list goes like this:

- Humor.

- Truth: This means self-awareness and honesty on
  both sides.

- Hygiene: That is, "good hygiene."

- Flexibility: I don't care about the physical flexibility. If I fall in love with somebody in a wheelchair,
  I'm not going to be pissed that he is in a wheelchair.
  I want somebody who is flexible in his thinking,
  somebody who is not close-minded.

- Variety, by which I mean someone who is interesting and open to new things, someone who has a lot of interests and has a multifaceted personality.

- An adult: This doesn't mean someone who is eighteen or over. It means someone who is a grown-up in that he has lived and learned and knows himself and has a sense of how the world works and can deal with it.

- Independence: someone who is not codependent or dependent on me financially or emotionally. I want someone who is their own person and confident in who they are, which leads to the most important thing:

- A fully formed person.

Mind you, these are the things that are important to me. They may not be important to you. So, I'll tell you what, I'll let you spend some time thinking about this.

Of course, you should also think about the things that you *don't* want. For example, it might be someone who is lazy, someone who puts you down or is dismissive of your ambitions or dreams, someone who is too needy, who doesn't want you to hang out with your friends, someone who has a drinking problem, who isn't reliable, who doesn't show up physically or emotionally when you need him.

There are probably a million things you *don't* want. Be clear and be specific. Don't wait until the honeymoon to figure it out. Spell it out for yourself now, because once you articulate all this stuff and are very clear before you meet someone, you will know what you are willing to deal with and not deal with. That way, you won't let chemistry or attraction or lust or wishful thinking get you into a relationship that you know isn't right for you. You will look at this new person and say, "Hey, you are hot and fun and I like hanging out with you but...you don't have that ability for deep connection that I really need, and you're always texting at the restaurant instead of talking to me, and I don't want that."

So get it down on paper, and force yourself to be clear about what is acceptable and what isn't. This will make you really think about it, and you'll also have it written down, so in the future you can look at it and remind yourself, "Oh shit, I said I didn't want that and yet here I am with someone who has that," or "I know I need such-and-such in order to be really happy with someone, and I'm just not getting it from this person."

Just write them down. I'll wait.

Five Things I Want in a Relationship

1) _____

2) _____

3) _____

4) _____

5) _____

Five Things I Cannot Tolerate in a Relationship

1) _____

2) _____

3) _____

4) _____

5) _____

Oh good, you're back.

So you wrote the two lists. Now let me ask you a question: Do you have the patience to wait for what you're looking for? Most people don't. Most people will rush into a relationship because they feel lonely, or they want to share the holidays with somebody, or they want a vacation with somebody. Or, as some people who will remain nameless have done, they get married just because they really like the wedding and party, love the idea of everyone coming together and saying, "This is a really great day."

Yeah, that last one was me.

Yes, I'll admit it, I loved all that. It was the day to day I couldn't handle. I'd wake up and look over to the person next to me in bed and think, "Oh, damn, you're still here." That was my attitude. You can't have that attitude with someone you profess to want to marry or live with. Or even date. You have to decide if you are really ready to be with one other person.

I guess by now it's pretty obvious that I do not like being married or in a relationship, except for the two or three minutes that I'm interested in it. Sometimes it's because of the little things.

If I want to, I can...well, I'll put it frankly, fart walking through the house, and I don't have to explain it to someone. If it smells really bad, I don't have to say I'm sorry. Maybe I have to say I'm sorry to the cat, but that's the only creature I have to deal with.

If I want to, I can drop something on the floor and not pick it up until tomorrow. I feel okay about that. I don't have to talk to anyone if I don't feel like it. I can hear my own thoughts.

This freedom for me is worth far more than any relationship.

I have to be honest with myself about all this because sometimes I used to walk around in a fog, thinking, "Oh, this person likes me. I'd better hook up with him."

I can tell you: it's not a good idea to do that. It *is* a good idea to take your time. Most people don't want to do that because they want instantaneous relief. They're feeling all sad, thinking, "I'm lonely, boohoo. I have to go find somebody."

I need you to understand that it's okay to want to be by yourself.

It's okay to be patient and hold out for what you really want in a relationship.

There's no reason to settle. Sometimes that means spending some time with yourself and figuring out what you're looking for—*not* what your family or your friends or community or society dictate to you, but what *you* really, deep down in your heart and soul as a freethinking individual, want.

A big part of what drives many of us is women would love to be someone's muse. We want to be the person who stirs creativity in the person she's with. I don't know if guys have that as much as women do, but the idea of trying to find that person you can inspire, whose creativity you spark so that he can create amazing things, and you're just hip and wonderful and you're living in this great bubble of happiness...well, I can tell you it just doesn't happen all that often.

Once I realized that being someone's muse and inspiring him to greatness probably wasn't going to be my life, I took a good hard look at what I was getting out of relationships and came to understand three things about myself:

1. I should not ever live with anyone, because I just don't have the patience for it. I'm very cranky around other people.

2. If I'm looking for someone whom I can spark, it can take a really, really, really long time, so perhaps continuing to look for that, or trying to

manufacture that, is not the smartest thing and is a waste of my time and efforts that could be better spent elsewhere.

3. I want to be my own damn muse, not someone else's.

Now, if I had been paying closer attention in my youth, I would have known that I don't enjoy being with anybody hour to hour. I don't want somebody with me all the time.

When I first got married, I was young—too young—and I thought that getting married was what "normal" people did. I also had big dreams, even though it may have seemed ridiculous to other people at the time. I did pull it together, though, didn't I?

Everyone else wanted me to be something smaller than what I was. They didn't know how powerful my dreams were. I was supposed to be a good wife and mother, and go to work and make money doing the most boring job imaginable (at least to me). The marriage was doomed from the start because I was never that person. I didn't want somebody laughing at my dreams and hopes, or taking the liberty to tell me what I should be instead of asking me what I wanted to be.

But back then, I didn't know that it would have been okay to say, "You know what? I don't want the kind of relationship where you get to tell me what I'm supposed to be and I have to listen to you and put my own desires on the back burner. The way I see it, we're equals. I want this and this. What do you want? Okay, now let's see if we can work it out so we are both happy."

No, I just went from zero to one hundred. Got married, had a baby—and I loved her as soon as I met her, as soon as she emerged from me. I liked being pregnant, but the part between being pregnant and holding the baby was pretty horrible. I guess it's a shock to most women. And back in those days, when your water broke, they put you in a room by yourself, and then sometimes a nurse would come in and yell at you to stop making so much noise, because all you were doing was pushing a basketball through the eye of a needle.

Back then, nurses were quite nasty. Nowadays, you have a party in the delivery room, but not when I became a mom. That's why I never wanted to have another kid. No, thank you. That whole process was not a pleasant experience.

Where were we?

Finally, I couldn't avoid it any longer. I kept coming back to the truth, what my gut was telling me: I didn't really want to be married. I liked the idea of what it promised. Who wouldn't? When you get married, people are so incredibly supportive, and they have the best expectations for you. Not just the family and friends who all idealize marriage as the be-all and end-all, but also the person you're marrying. It's a time when things are fresh and everyone is optimistic. That optimism and hope kind of drove me to make some of the choices I made in my life. But my choices should not reflect badly on the people I chose to be with. It really was, and is, all me—which is why I just don't get married anymore.

The only way I would want to be in a relationship at this point is if I could find someone who was willing to live in another state. Then I would see him when I wanted, and that would be perfect. That person is not out there for me right now, though.

I'm good with that, even if it freaks a lot of people out.

Relationships are by definition not just about you. There's another person involved, and he or she has 50 percent of that relationship, and you've got to be able to transcend all the bullshit and work at it. This is something I've never been able to master, which is why I suck at relationships.

I'm just being honest.

I don't suck so much now, because I *am* so honest with myself. I draw a line in the sand, which is basically, "If you come to me and who you are or who I've seen you to be isn't comfortable for me, I am going to cut it off. Right now." I am not going to wait three, four, five, six years. I am not going to try and pretend that I'm happy when I'm not or think I'm going to change or fix someone.

When I was growing up, things were different. Women

were raised to have their highest purpose in life be to get married, and that there was a cultural expectation that the man would work and pay for things while the woman had the babies and took care of the man and the house.

Today, things have changed. But we haven't caught up with all the changes. Look at the way things are now: Despite the fact that women make their own money, have their independence, and are exposed to so many ideas, you would think we'd think twice about this marriage thing and not still look at it as the ultimate goal. So many women still do, though, and we go into these marriages with expectations that don't make sense, and that we don't even articulate to one another. Both men and women do this.

As they say, the more things change, the more they stay the same

So when I say, "You've got to be up front," I mean be up front with *yourself*. Also be up front with the other person. Don't even think for a second, "Well, I can change him," because you really can't change people unless they are determined to change, or if they are already in the midst of changing. Otherwise, you are going to be disappointed, and then you're mad, and the relationship is going south, and you're still walking down the aisle.

That's not good. That's a combustible situation.

Before one of my weddings—I'm not saying which one—my mother pulled me aside and said, "Here are the car keys. You know you don't want to get married. Get in the car and leave."

Did I listen to her? The answer is no.

I said, "We invited all these people to the wedding. I can't just leave."

So I got married anyway, which makes me kind of an asshole, because I knew the truth, and I went around it.

So I'm trying to help people not do that.

Tell yourself what you want. Check your list. It may be that right now you just want to spend some time with yourself. Well, that's okay, in spite of what your friends and family will tell you.

It's okay to be single.

It's okay to feel like you want to be by yourself for a while.

Because the truth of the matter is—and don't tell anybody I told you this—not everyone is meant to be married.

Take me, for example. I am with other people most of my day, and I have a lot of stimulation from day to day. When I come home I want to relax, not interact with someone else or deal with his problems. I want some "me" time.

Once I realized that my needs could be met by me, life got a lot easier. Then other people didn't have to help me figure out what my life was. I already knew it.

Now, every now and then, I get a little urge—you know what I'm talking about—and I can make a phone call and have a friend come over.

But we're not talking about that right now.

Before I arrived at that place, though, I had to come to terms with the fact that I was all right.

There is nothing wrong with me for wanting to be alone or for being comfortable being alone. There is nothing wrong with having three or four cats if I decide to— but because I'm very vain and don't want people calling me a cat lady, I have only one. There's a lot of ego going around here, and it's all mine and I understand that.

I hope you see the foolishness of not being true to yourself. Believe me, I know it's very hard to do, when people are pushing you into getting married. Gay folks are having it the worst now, because everybody is "You can get married now. When are you going to get married?" But the question is: Why do you want to do that? Yes, you get some security from your other half, you share the finances, and if something happens to you and you get sick or can't work, you can fall back on what your spouse has, and blah, blah, blah.

But, fundamentally, what is the purpose of getting married?

Let's say some couple has been together for twenty-six years. Now, I don't think they need to go to a church and make it formal. Pretty much, they're married. As soon as those people who were together for twenty-six years get married, don't be surprised if they get a divorce.

Why? Because it feels like they have to live up to this list of what marriage is supposed to be, and they are not themselves anymore.

That's the answer to the other question: why people get divorced. The message we're getting doesn't make it clear that it's all right to be together for twenty-six years or thirty years or fifty years, gay or straight, and not be married. I'm telling you, it is okay. Then, if you decide, "You know what, this isn't the life I want anymore, I'm living a lie," then, as long as you're up front, it's all good. It won't be easy, but it will be a hell of a lot easier than if you are legally bound.

What do you do if the person you meet who can fulfill what you need happens to wear stinky cologne or a terrible thong? Well, where do you draw your line in the sand? What are you willing to accept? Are you willing to accept the fact that there's stinky cologne in your future? Or really bumpy-looking, bad-looking thongs? If you're willing to accept that because there are five hundred thousand other things in that person that you adore, that's your line in the sand. You can live with that, because you really think this person is terrific and maybe you can introduce him to some nice Armani or Tom Ford cologne, or buy her a nice smooth Wolford thong that actually works for her.

It's all about who you really want to be—which brings us to the next chapter.

Should You Go Out and Seek Love or Wait to See If It Comes to You?

Why not just live? That way, if it comes, you're great. If it doesn't come, you're great. Should you go out? If you want it, you can go look for it. We all need company at times, and we all need solitude at times. There is attraction, there is ego boost, there is sex, there is friendship and having fun with someone. But love? That isn't something that necessarily shows up because you want it to, and it can take time to build. So go live your life and do all the things that you want to do; don't wait for love to show up. When you are out there doing what you enjoy, it is more likely that love will show up.

CHAPTER SIX

Know Your Truth

P atience. Fortitude. Truth. Sometimes finding the right relationship can feel like searching for the Holy Grail. You have to be like a knight of the Round Table on his quest. You have to take your time, and you have to know your truth, and you can't settle for tarnished treasure or cheap imitations.

People tend to rush into relationships because they are afraid they are not going to have anybody, like that's a bad thing. Also, we're not a society that understands how important it is to be self-aware. It's fine to want to be with somebody, but you've got to figure out what you're looking for, instead of finding out what you don't want when you're in the middle of it. Like I said, I'm not a psychologist or psychiatrist, but it just seems to me that you have to make a bargain with yourself and tell your-self the truth.

You get into a relationship and you want to make the other person feel good or feel better about themselves, and as women we put our own needs or contributions or achievements on the back burner to stroke the man's ego. So you bullshit him at your own expense.

I started to see that trait in myself, but for a while I was too lazy to do anything about it. I would get into a relationship, and soon enough I would know it was bad. But I'd be so lazy that I wouldn't break it off. So three, four years later, I'm still there. Then, one day, I'm like, "I'm taking my toys and I'm going. It's been fun. See you! Bye."

But doing that is too much. So now I just cut them loose as soon as I know it's not going to work.

You need to say to yourself, "I'm going to wait and find the right person," instead of "Oh, I'm so lonely, I'm going to jump into anything." Look at this book as a brake. It's just a long, long brake, like in the old Volkswagen Bug. Pull up that brake, slow down, and give yourself time to find the right person.

At this point in my life I have three grandchildren, a daughter, a son-in-law, and now a great-grandchild. They take up a lot of my time. I have a terrific family, and I don't need a new one or another one. I have my career, which keeps me pretty busy, and I have all the other things I like to do with my time, the things that are bigger than me, like raising awareness about HIV/AIDS, education, homelessness. (You already know I also have a cat, an evil cat, and that that's really all I can handle at home at this point.)

So I have a lot of things going on. I also have myself and my relationship with myself, which is pretty important and helps keep all those other things going. So I know that bringing somebody in would require that I stop and think about yet another person. And that would probably be too much for me. Although a relationship can be a lot of fun in the beginning, in the end, it becomes too much responsibility.

I got to this place of knowing over time, from my life experience. It's because I have my family and my career set up. It's because I've made a lot of mistakes and have tried to learn from them. It's because I have learned to be honest with myself, have learned who I really am (normal), and I have accepted it. It's also because I don't buy into the media hype.

The thing I would say to everybody is "Stop letting the media tell you what you feel and what you think you need." It's just so stupid.

Like on *Gossip Girl*: they all have the best clothes and they have their cliques and they play games to get their man. "I'm going to do this, and then he will do that." Media and advertising are all about manipulating people.

In some ways, self-esteem has become a media creation. Yes, people have self-esteem, but then we're told, "Your self-esteem is not enough." We need to have certain clothes and toys and friends and behavior.

If you're lucky, you grow up like most kids. Some shit you know, some shit you don't. Some stuff is hard, some stuff is easy. You learn a lot, but you get better, and the mere fact that you're getting better lifts your self-esteem. Healthy self-esteem comes from learning new things and developing yourself. Not from having all the right stuff.

Now we've put it in people's minds that it's a *Gossip Girl* world. I don't know if it is, but I do know that if people stopped trying to live the dream of a movie or a TV show, stopped allowing pop culture to tell them what makes them worthy or gives them value, they would be a lot happier. Figure that stuff out on your own. When you do, you will be a more authentic you, and that will reflect how solid you are in your sense of self and in how you react to and behave with other people.

They say that you have to love yourself first before you can love somebody else. It's true. I have to love me, I have to have high self-esteem before I love somebody else. It's really simple.

If you don't love yourself, and you're loving somebody else, you're putting all the responsibility for yourself on him, which is not fair. Everybody has to come in 100 percent. I'm here 100 percent. You're here 100 percent. We will work through whatever we find. But if you're coming in as basically half a person, any relationship is not going to work. Nobody should be in charge of babysitting you, or vice versa. Once you are a grown-up, you no longer need a babysitter, and you should not be babysitting your friends or your lovers. You should both be self-sufficient people who know themselves and who can share that with each other. That is called maturity.

One of my favorite books is Rainer Maria Rilke's *Letters to a Young Poet*. In it, he talks about the importance of two people in a relationship remaining separate individuals and being whole people before they get into anything. Here's a quote from the book that captures some of it:

> [A] good marriage is one in which each partner appoints the other to be the guardian of his solitude, and thus they show each other the greatest possible trust. A merging of two people is an impossibility... [O]nce the realization is accepted that even between the closest people infinite distances exist, a marvelous living side-by-side can grow up for them, if they succeed in loving the expanse between them, which gives them the possibility of always seeing each other as a whole and before an immense sky.

Again, the best kind of relationship is one where two whole people come together and support one another. Rilke does not say the best kind of relationship is one where you are going to try to fix the other person and mold him into what you think you want.

He has a lot of other interesting things to say, so when you're done with this book, go out and get his. He said it a hundred years before I did.

How, you may ask, do you know if the person you are involved with is coming into the relationship as half a person? You will know when the person you're with is not quiet—he (or she!) acts like a baby or is very needy, "Give me, give me, give me." When it's all about him (or her). Why is he so needy? He hasn't yet learned how to fulfill himself, his own needs. This takes self-awareness and maturity.

But, again, the specter of being alone pops up, and we go, "No, no, no. I can work it out. I can teach him. I can make him better."

I am here to tell you that you can't. You can't fix someone else. You've got to be honest and say, "No, I understand. You need a lot of stuff."

And I ask you, why would you *want* to "fix" another person anyway?

Why would you want to fix your lover, your friend?

And why would you want to marry someone and attach yourself to him if he needs to be fixed?

The only reason is because you need to feel like a hero, you need to feel needed, and if that's the case, you aren't a complete person.

This is what gets us all into trouble.

Think about it. You have all sorts of other things going on in your life, and now you have to take care of this other person who doesn't know how to take care of himself. It is a lot of pressure, and while it may be some sort of ego boost in the short run, in the long run it is going to drain you and take away whatever attraction or respect you had for him.

You need to realize that this is not the person for you, because instead of adding to your life, he is subtracting. Getting to this point isn't easy because it means telling yourself the truth, and that takes some practice. It's all about the truth that you have to tell to yourself. It's the hardest thing to do, because usually people just want things to work out. They don't want to be disappointed. They are willing to settle. You only get one life, though, so I ask, why?

Be honest with yourself and be patient.

While it may seem that it takes a lifetime to figure this stuff out, that it's an "ongoing process," that you learn through experience and mistakes—I say that's bullshit.

People know what they need. When somebody says something and it kinds of hurts you, you know this might not be the person for you. Even a child knows when she doesn't feel right, when she isn't being respected or loved the way she wants to be. But we all want to be accepted, to be loved, sometimes so badly that we let things slide. But you let things slide for too long and soon enough you are living a lie.

We've been talking about living your truth, which you know at the core of your being.

We've been talking about how you have to speak honestly to yourself. If you can't tell yourself the truth, who can you tell the truth to? Why should I believe you if you're lying to yourself?

Is this getting too deep for you?

Are you still not sure about what I'm saying?

Are you asking, "But how do you know?"

The most important thing is that you have to listen to your truths, desires, and wants. And you have to believe you deserve all of it.

Or you need to just be honest with yourself about your own choices and say, "Yes, I'm going to settle and just go with any Jane, Dick, or Harry."

Or "You know what? I'm going to wait. I'm going to see how this goes. I'm going to find somebody that really makes me say, 'Hey, now,' who captures my attention and keeps me interested and stimulated for more than a minute."

One of the things I hear all the time on *The View* is that women think they either don't have time or can't spend time working on themselves or deepening their relationship with themselves. I'm writing this book in part as a response to a lot of that kind of nonsense.

What are you talking about? If you're not together as a human being, you're not good for anybody. So you've got to take care of yourself. Take the time to get to know yourself. Who are you? What do you want? You have to commit yourself to answering these questions, even if it takes a while.

Sometimes I just cannot believe my ears. The same issues keep coming up again and again in our discussions on *The View*, and the things coming out of people's mouths are so weird.

Like the reasons that some people get into relationships—which to me often seem like all the wrong reasons. Maybe these people were trying to be funny, but what I have heard is so consistent that it really started to bother me.

I thought, "How can so many people have such wrong ideas about what is going to make them happy?"

I kept seeing people behaving in ways that I knew

was not going to help them be happy in their relationships, acting in ways and holding on to ideas that weren't helping them.

By now I hope it's clear that you'd better take time for yourself, you'd better have a strong relationship with yourself, and you'd better take care of yourself. Take care of your life. It's the most important thing and it is from there, that core of your relationship with yourself, that all other relationships spring.

When I've been in relationships, most of the time I was trying to find that point of "normal," which I've already talked about. Everybody tells you that this is what you're supposed to do. But what if you're not that person? What if you are independent and evolved and willing to commit to your own truth? This is who this book is for: someone who has a lot of responsibilities and lots of things going on in her life and in her mind and in her heart.

So, for me, I have my family, my work, my passions and causes, and I am committed to all of them. A relationship has to fit into and work *within that.*

And I have me. And you have you, your own self, and your own very full life.

I think that that is what you should be doing: leading your own fulfilling life, learning new things, working on your career, your friends and family, your causes and passions. Instead of sitting around waiting for some guy to call, go develop yourself.

The craziest thing is—and I don't know when women forgot, and it's particular to women—women forgot that relationships don't mean anything if you're not solid. Another thing I hear on the show all the time that I don't understand is when women say, "I can't have it all." But you *can*. Are you talking about some movie you saw that was about having it all? You can actually have your career, have your kid, have your passions. Yes, you're going to be a little tired, you're going to be stretched thin, you're going to need some help once in a while, because it really does take a village. None of us is a machine. You're going to have these issues, but that's part of it.

Real life is much more complicated than any movie, and that's as it should be. If you're doing things that you believe in or that are making you happy or fulfilling you, as exhausted as you might be, you do it because this is your one life. You are doing what you want to do.

Nobody said it was going to be easy, but a full life isn't supposed to be easy. If you want to just sit on the couch and waste your life, go right ahead, but don't think that with some magic wand your life is going to fix itself without your involvement and energy, and don't think a man is going to come knocking on your door and fix it all for you.

It must be very hard for people, because everybody

is scared for some reason. Scared especially that they are not going to find somebody to spend the rest of their life with. But the point of all this is: I don't know if you're *supposed* to. I don't know if you *want* to spend the rest of your life just thinking about that. I would run from that.

The question of "What do I want in my life?" is important. Figure out what you want in a person. Just in a friend. The same criteria you have for friendship should be the same criteria you have for a relationship.

Do I want to hang out with you?

Do I want to spend time with you?

There are a lot of folks who hang with people they hate. I don't understand this. Perhaps, just perhaps, it's fear of being alone.

This book isn't saying, "This is the only way." It's saying, "This is a way that makes sense to me." Maybe it will make sense to you.

You can try all the other stuff you want to. Expectations? You can shoot them up to the moon, but the only person that will be disappointed is you, because you'll know if somebody is meeting or not meeting your expectations.

What do you do if and when they stop? Then it's like, "What did I do? Who am I? Where am I?"

No. Walking into a relationship with high expectations is not a good idea.

There are a lot of the books out there telling women how to snare a man, with all the tricks you can use to get a man and keep him. But where is the book telling women to be happy in themselves, and to figure out what they want, and to become the people they want to be so that any relationship that comes out from that is based on a real connection, a real friendship, between two whole people?

So I see this book as telling people how to snare a partner for longer than we see most relationships last. After all, this is all about carefully crafting a way to find somebody you like.

The last thing I want to say in this chapter is I want to invite people to be as inventive in finding the relationships they want in their life as they are in finding prom dresses and ways to propose to people. Put that much energy in it. Be as discerning when you're looking for people to have in your life. Take that much time to do it. That's my opinion.

So go, take a bathroom break. I'll wait for you.

If You Sat Your Granddaughter Down and Could Share Only Three Qualities to Look for in a Life Partner, What Would They Be?

It's a hard question for me to answer because, again, I feel like what works for me may not work for other people. And if you've read this far, you know that I don't necessarily approach these things the same way other people do.

I know that I would tell her to look for honesty, humor, and kind of a twinkle. That twinkle, that spark that means someone is engaged in his life and enjoying himself. That he is somebody who is adventurous, interested in experiencing things in life instead of just being interested in things, someone you can have real conversations with.

I believe conversation gives you a lot of insight into how comfortable you are with the person you're with. That's why dating is important, as well as spending real time with someone, not just a month or even a year. It may take maybe two years, maybe three years with somebody to figure out if this is somebody you want to hang out with long term. If you hang out with him for only a year and then you get married, you're sort of stuck.

I don't understand why people are always in such a rush to get married. I say take your time, look at the qualities of this person. Do they meet your criteria for what you are looking for in a partner? That's the thing that is most important.

But I can't tell my granddaughter or you what is going to make you happy. I can only tell you what works for me. So that's why in this book, there is lots of discussion going on about various things. Why we feel the way we feel. Why we are accepting of something. Is it because we haven't been

with the person long enough to find out
what his bad or not interesting qualities are?

You kind of have to spend some real
quality time with someone to come to know
him, so that's probably the advice I would
give: Spend some time with this person. See
if he really gives you what you're looking for.
Who knows? Maybe you're supposed to be
with him for only three months.

We fall in love so fast because people
feel like "If I don't do it now, I'm never going
to have it," but that's not true. It might take
you a long time to find a relationship. But if
it takes you a long time to find it, maybe it
will last longer.

That's how I think, anyway.

Is It Okay to Have Secrets from Your Past That You Do Not Wish to Share with Your Current Partner?

You kind of have to ask yourself, "How would I feel if I discovered my partner used to be [fill in your own blank]?" It really depends on what kind of secret it is. If you've had five kids and they're living in another state and you go and say, "Oh I'm just going to be a lifeguard in the state of XYZ," and you're really going to go take care of your kids because you have a whole separate life there, I don't know if that's a good secret. I don't know if it's good to have secrets from somebody you're actually trying to have a life with because it always will hang on you.

On the other hand, I don't recommend sharing everything at once with people. After some time, say three to four years, when you find that this is the person you're going to stay with or you hope to stay with, then it's a pretty good idea to tell him the thing that you are the most afraid of someone finding out.

You know that if you're afraid of somebody finding out, that's the one thing he's going to find out, because you're going to subconsciously make it happen. You're going to somehow cause this information to come out, and then you're going to be all freaked out.

So, secrets are not good, but don't reveal them in the first five minutes of a relationship. If you're going to have children with somebody, though, and you've had DNCs or an abortion, or two or three, or a doctor has said it's going to be difficult for you to have children because of XYZ, you might want to share that. If you're someone who leaves hair all over the place because you actually wear a wig and he doesn't know it, it's good to tell him so he doesn't stumble on you looking like Lex Luthor.

I just think it's important to time your reveals.

WHOOPI'S SUGGESTED RULES FOR DAILY CIVILITY

Some time ago I wrote a book on manners that was meant to be for children, but now that I think about it, grown-ups could use one, too, especially when it comes to interacting with the people closest to them.

How you behave out in the world with strangers is a whole different book, but sometimes when we are in a close relationship with someone we can start taking them for granted or start being lazy about the way we treat them. This is what I mean when I say a relationship is work.

If you want to be in a relationship you can't be lazy. You need to be nice to the people closest to you, whether it's your parents, children, friends, or lovers.

Here are some basic rules:

- Do not text or use your phone at the dinner table.
- Do not answer your phone or respond to texts when you are in the middle of a conversation with an actual person in the

room. I have a friend whose boyfriend found it impossible not to answer his phone every time it rang: in restaurants, in the middle of conversations, when they were walking down the street together. She didn't like it, but she put up with it, and to me that was a big red flag. Why was the person calling more important than the person he was sitting having dinner with? I can only hope he didn't answer his texts or phone during sex. Unless it is a life-and-death situation or emergency, do not pick up the phone until after the meal or call the person back when your other conversation is done. You may not mean to do it, but checking your phone when you are with a flesh-and-blood person belittles the person you're with, it makes him feel he's not important enough to you for you to have some basic courtesy.

- Clean up after yourself, whether you are a guest or living with someone or just visiting his home. Do not treat the people around you like they are your house-keepers. Take your hair out of the drain yourself.

- Put the toilet seat down. Replace the toilet paper roll. Nobody wants to get their ass wet when they fall into the toilet in the dark in the middle of the night. And nobody wants to have to leave their ass wet because there's no toilet paper.

- Use your words, your nice words: *please, thank you, excuse me, you're welcome.*

- Don't use your bathroom words unless absolutely necessary, and don't use words that are disrespectful, belittling, or that make someone feel small or stupid. No name calling.

- Knock on the door before entering. You never really know what is going on behind a closed door. Maybe the person behind it is dancing around and singing like Tom Cruise in *Risky Business* and letting off a little steam. Or maybe he is enjoying some self-love. He doesn't want you barging in on him. Even when you live with someone, try to respect his privacy.

- Don't talk with food in your mouth. And if you get Dorito crumbs in the bed, please brush them off.
- Cover your mouth when coughing or sneezing.
- Don't interrupt when the other person is talking. It means you aren't listening to what she is saying.
- Know when and how to apologize. A simple "I'm sorry I blah blah blah'd" can usually do the trick for the small, day-to-day things. The bigger things need a much bigger apology.
- Tell the truth.
- Be kind. Just because you know how to push someone's buttons doesn't mean you have to push them.
- Treat your lovers like the friends they are.

CHAPTER SEVEN

And in the Beginning...

The beginning of any relationship is that romantic, unrealistic, infatuated, sex-crazed state when you and your new love are sitting in a bubble bath with soft music and candles, drinking champagne, and staring into each other's eyes. You're sending flowers and candies and little love notes, and your heart beats fast every time you hear from him, every time you see him. You take out a second mortgage on your house to pay for your new lingerie habit. The two of you don't leave the bedroom for days. It's all excitement and romance and anticipation. And it feels wonderful.

Ahhhh. This is the fun part. And we all love it. But...

I hate to burst your bubble, but while the beginning is

heavenly, unfortunately it has nothing to do with reality. It's all that stuff that, after six or seven months, you're no longer doing. You're not still sending the card every week or leaving the little love note on the pillow. Or waking up and kissing the person before you brush your teeth.

The beginning of any relationship is truly a heightened state, and it really is the fun part. Whether it's your relationship with your first baby, whether it's your relationship with your first boyfriend or girlfriend, or with your new friend. Everything is heightened. So you want to put the most bullshittian information out there so he doesn't go away. Since you are in this heightened state of excitement, you are being your very best self, a self that you probably aren't even close to actually being, and you are putting out your very best effort, and going the extra mile to maintain that heightened state. In the first blush of a relationship, you're wearing your favorite clothes. You have a new lacy thong for every day of the week. But you're not really being you—and believe me, neither is the other person. It's all bullshit, and I'm sorry to be the one to tell you, but it isn't going to last.

Now, we're talking about relationships between adults. If we're talking about the relationship you have with your first baby, then no, you're not you. Your stomach has just been huge and you don't know what to do, but you're so glad to get that thing out of there. That first baby—you treat him like he's perfect and precious. By your second baby, you are throwing that second baby around and not obsessing over every little burp and diaper. That's because you know what you are doing this time around and you knew what to expect and were prepared. You are more yourself.

Anytime you begin a relationship, it's a first relationship. Well, the first time you feel love it's for the person who's carrying you around in her arms. That's the first love of your life–if you're lucky enough to have a parent anyway. Not everybody gets to have that. When you're a little kid, love is comfort, love is the person who takes care of you.

Then you have your first love, puppy or young love:

"You make me feel good."
"I heard you like me."
"I think I like you."
"I like your shoes."
"I like your book."
"I want to be with you."
"I want to have a boyfriend."
"I want to have a girlfriend."

Or whatever. Relationships are pretty much all the same when we are young and when they are new, at least until we become devious about them.

In a new relationship with an adult, even when it's your second time around or your one-hundredth time around, you revert to some idealized version of yourself for a short period, perhaps to relive those original puppy loves or out of hope that you are really the wonderful person your new love thinks you are. You are not who you truly are, but rather a heightened version. The version that is the person in all those songs I was talking about earlier. The "Good Morning" and the "(You Make Me Feel Like) A Natural Woman." *That's* who you are. For a short period you get to be the girl in the movie, and you are the girl in the song, and trying to get that feeling, experiencing it, is such a high that it becomes like a drug. It's why all those songs and movies are written: to capture that elusive, short-lived feeling that some people—and in my youth I might have been one of those people—think love is supposed to feel like. It is being in love with love.

To you, the other person can do no wrong. Nothing he does is odd. It's all cute. It's all really cute.

In the beginning, when you're with that new person, you can't let go of the fart, right? Then, when you've been with someone forever, you will let it go and stink up the room and you don't care, but in the beginning you're holding it in. If one little poop comes out, it's cute. "Oh, a stinky!" Four years from now it's like, "What the fuck was that?"

I always say be yourself from the very beginning. So I will let one rip, and then I will always know if the relationship is going to go past a week. It's like saying, "If we're going to be living together or spending a lot of time together, there are some things you are just going to have to deal with." Now, I'm not going to go and fart at the restaurant, but I am going to tell you when I get up to go to the bathroom, "I'm going to go fart, because I can't fart here." To me, that's natural.

I know lots of people who will never, ever fart in front of the person they are with. Maybe that's how they were raised, but not me. I'm a farter. I like to be comfortable. But I have learned in my life places to fart and places not to fart. If you're in my bed, for instance, you have to follow my rules. The only bad part about all this is that my bedmate also has the same freedom. This is why I'm alone. Because I don't *want* him to have the same freedom.

But that's neither here nor there.

The first blush of a relationship makes you so different. Your friends are looking at you trying to figure out what's going on, because the change is happening. You're not as schlubby as you were, maybe. Or you're wearing more adornment. You're better scented. And you walk differently. You walk like "I'm walking on sunshine, oh-ohhhhhhh." It's all great, and Bambi is coming up and eating right out of your hand, and little butterflies are flying around, and birds are singing. He or she—or they, depending on if you're in a threesome—has a halo over them. They are, in those early days, perfection.

A lot of this is just a chemical reaction. All those endorphins and dopamine create a different kind of energy. Chemical reaction or not, though, no one tells the truth in the beginning. You don't dress that way all the time. You don't smell like that all the time. You don't have wear expensive, completely impractical lingerie all the time. You don't look like that all the time. You don't comb your hair that often. I can attest to that.

This chemical reaction part subsides much sooner than two or three years. I think it can even subside after a few months.

Do people mistake that newness as love, and are so quick to say, "I love you"? Yes, they do. After all, we've been programmed to say those words, that it is the next natural thing that's supposed to happen in this situation. You meet somebody and have fun with him and really like him and have some nice sex, and then, in a short amount of time, you tell him you love him.

It is a mistake to confuse love with chemistry, or love with that heightened state of infatuation in the beginning. But a lot of people think that's what love is, and when that initial period is over, so is the relationship. They can't go to the next level, which is the real level.

I'll bet if you asked people to describe what love means to them or what love is to them, very few people could do it.

People mistake love for "I really like being with you."
People mistake love for "We have great times in bed."
People mistake love for "I need you to protect me."
And people mistake love for "You take care of me."

Then, if they stick around, it gets a little weird, because then your face starts to slip. Your whole persona starts to slip. You're back in the stinky pants. Maybe you're not as hygienically scented as you'd like to be, or as you were before, so your odor changes. You are wearing your granny pants underwear and a stretched-out bra. And now you're sort of getting used to how we do this.

The first time you're in bed with somebody, you're very nervous and, you know, wondering who is going to start and "What should we do?"

"Oh my God, I can't believe this is happening, how do I look? And blah, blah, blah. Then you figure out whether you're compatible in the bed. Again, in the beginning, your expectations are very high because everything tells you that you've met that special person, so you figure everything else is going to be perfect as well.

But what do you do if that doesn't work as well as you want it to? You want to train him, don't you? There are these expectations that you hope the sex is going to be as good as all the romance or the feelings. So you say, "Well, if the sex isn't great, then I'll have to teach him."

You know if somebody can't satisfy you. You know it.

So you need to show him what to do. And you do it in a way that doesn't make him feel like he's an idiot. You do it like, "Let's try this…let's try that…what do you like…what do I like?"

But the first blush is really sort of "Oh my God, this is great and wonderful." "Gee, am I going to be his muse?" "Am I going to be this or that?" It's all that movie shit.

I don't know when movies changed—I don't know if they have, really. But I don't remember a lot of these issues hitting folks in the 1950s and such. Maybe they were. But you had to meet people one on one, or you had pen pals or whatever. Everything took longer. You had to physically go somewhere to meet the person. You had to get to know each other over a period of time. Or, in some places, the parents arranged the marriage and you went along with it, which is maybe also a good idea for people. Not my favorite thing, but some people find it really helpful because you grow together. You are forced to get to know each other and figure it out.

Times have changed. I remember reading about Barbra Streisand and when she started her relationship with James Brolin. She was away somewhere making a movie—they were in different countries—and she was in the hotel room in the bathroom on the floor, and for hours and hours they spoke on the phone.

People don't do that anymore.

When I was growing up, I could be on the phone with

my best friends or boyfriends for hours and hours, and it created a connection, a trust, a common language that was important. You just liked hearing the sound of the other person's voice.

Today everyone texts, and something has been lost. That connection isn't given a chance to develop when your main form of communication is texting. And texts can be so easily misunderstood and are valued not for being honest but for being cute or clever. All human interaction has been reduced to emojis. Don't get me wrong, emojis can be cute, but they don't begin to create a connection that gets two people closer. They are more like a shorthand type of language.

So a connection is built not through emojis but through intimacy. The official definition of *intimacy* is that it's a close, familiar, and usually affectionate or loving personal relationship. It is an understanding of who the other is and creates nice familiarity, warmth, affection. Not necessarily love, but intimacy can certainly lead to love.

But this definition is a little vague, isn't it? A little stiff. It sounds good, but what does it really mean to you?

Think about your own definition of intimacy, which can probably start with some of the things you want in a relationship. Spelling out your definition of intimacy is taking that to the next level:

My Definition of Intimacy

*IS:*_____

_____

_____

_____

_____

_____

_____

_____

The other thing about relationships—and this goes not just for sexual relationships, but relationships in general—is the less interaction you have with people, the harder a relationship with another person is going to be.

It's very easy to make friends or fall in love with an avatar. It's like falling in love with a character in a book. It's not real. You don't really know this person.

Today, the hardest thing people have to contend with is how to hang out socially. People don't know how to talk on the phone. They don't know how to talk on the iPhone or the A phone or the LMNOP phone or the smartphone or the dumbphone. Because no one has time. And certain social skills and ways to connect are being lost.

Social media have created a whole different way of interacting than what we did years ago, where the phone would ring, you would have to ask your mother can you talk on the phone, and then you would sit and have a conversation. Or you'd sit there waiting for the phone to ring. Was he going to call? Wasn't he going to call? Now it's just you text. Everything is a text. Or you wait for an e-mail from somebody. Nobody really has to put themselves out there in an honest or a vulnerable way.

And don't get me started on online profiles. They're basically marketing tools.

And then there are these apps—in the gay world, there's Grindr and Scruff, where you go onto your app and you can see who is in your neighborhood or who is five feet away or ten feet away, and you can either hook up with or talk to that person, but it's all in an app and you can pretend and hide behind it.

For the straight world there's Tinder, where you look at a bunch of photos and swipe, swipe, swipe, until you find someone whose looks you like, and then if that person swipes you back, you can hook up. But you don't even know anything about one another. It's a superficial connection at best.

Remember, in the very beginning, we talked about patience. Patience is required to have a relationship, a human relationship, a human interaction with someone else. It also means you cannot be self-absorbed. You have to pay attention to the person you're talking to. That's whether you are going to be friends or lovers or whatever. But generally, once you get past all the electronics, you still have to do the flesh on flesh. You still have to meet. You still have to connect somehow in a way that is real and meaningful if you are going to make a real friend.

Take a look at how you defined intimacy in that exercise I gave you. I'm guessing you will agree with me that creating intimacy with another person can happen only through face-to-face connection over time.

Because, even beyond good sex and good companionship, people still crave intimacy. Not just physical intimacy, although we all certainly crave that, but emotional intimacy. It's what makes us feel alive, makes us feel human. In the beginning of a relationship, sexual chemistry can seem to be intimacy, but understanding one another and the ability to share and connect take time to create. And they require a certain amount of vulnerability and honesty.

So while lots of people find relationships on the Internet, it's hard to know if you're going to connect with that person. I like a good old-fashioned bar, because I want to know how you smell. I want to see you. Not because I want to see if you're cute, but to see if you're crazy.

There is a movie called *Looking for Mr. Goodbar*, where Diane Keaton's character goes to this bar every night and picks up these edgy guys. One night she goes home with this really handsome, seemingly charming guy and then…well, let's just say it doesn't end well for her. You could say, "Oh, that was just a movie." But it was based on a true story. It happens.

I will never forget that movie, because now I feel like I need to really know who a person. I need to see the person. I need to see you in the daylight where other people are, which is the way you should meet any new person. You need to be around other people when you meet new people because you don't know if you're meeting Norman Bates. Or Mr. Goodbar. You just never know.

Something you should know is everybody is Googleable now. So if your friends Google the guy you're with, or the girl you're with, or the man you're with, or whomever, and they say, "Hey, this doesn't look too good. This person seems a little sketchy," don't say, "No, no, that won't happen with me." And don't cut your friends loose or cut them dead, because they are your friends and they're just trying to protect you. So when you meet a new person, you might want to Google him and see what's out there about this person. It doesn't mean that it's true, but it tells you there's something you need to know, because if everyone else can see what you're finding online, they're going to start asking you questions, and you should probably be asking those same questions. You need to get in front of these stories.

That's life. You don't really know until you know. Somebody gives his best face in the first five months of the relationship. Everything is fantastic, and then one day you have that disagreement, that first disagreement. If you're lucky, it will just be like, "Oh, well, no, I never thought about that in that way." "I don't know *why* you didn't think about it. *I* thought about it." Instead of "No, I never thought about that" and *slap!* "Well, you think about it now. "Then you have a real decision to make.

So you don't know until you know. That's why you have to be present in the relationship and pay attention to what is actually happening, instead of living in some fantasy world or world of denial. You have to be present. Red flags are there for a reason. And you have to look straight at them. See those red flags. Listen to your gut. If your gut is screaming, "No, no, no, Mr. Bill, no, Mr. Bill," like that clay guy from *Saturday Night Live*—well, you need to listen to that and act accordingly.

How can I say this with such authority? It's because, in my lifetime, I've ignored enough red flags to fill the country of China. I would be Oprah by now if I had paid attention to some of those red flags, but I didn't.

How Do You Deal with Your Partner's Friends When They Are Scumbags?

One person's scumbag is another person's friend. So you have to kind of figure out what constitutes a scumbag in your mind and what does it mean to the relationship.

You don't like his friends? That's one thing.

You don't like his friends because you're jealous because they're spending too much time together? That's another thing.

You don't like his friends because they're leading him down paths that are ultimately going to be bad for him, at least in your opinion, and you're not allowed to say anything? Perhaps you're with the wrong person.

It's hard to know, because everybody's scumbag is different. Sorry.

What Do You Think About Age Differences?

If you are twenty years older than your boy-friend, I say stop talking about it and just have a good time. When it comes to age, sometimes there are things that you discover you can't do. I don't mean physical things you can't do. I mean there are things you just can't deal with.

I had a guy who was much younger than me, and he did not know that Paul McCart-ney had another band called the Beatles. He had known only about Wings. And it was like, "WHAT?"

So you have to look at that and see where you can connect and where you can't. And you adapt, as well as you are able to. You find things where you connect and parlay that into something. The things that you can't connect on, you can educate the other person, and he can do the same with you.

Younger people will teach you how to do stuff, too. So it's never a bad idea to have younger people in the mix. Just saying.

Why Do People Think Not Arguing Is a Healthy Sign?

I don't know why people think that. Not all relationships play out the same way. Not all couples argue, and maybe that's what drew those two people together. They talk stuff out and they don't argue. It's healthy for them.

It's not healthy for everybody, but I don't think there's any blanket statement that is true about relationships. There's not one answer; there are many. One person's prince is another one's pauper. People feel the way they feel for lots of different reasons. There are some people who don't argue who have been together for thirty years, and you argue with your partner and you've been together only four years. Maybe there's something to be said for it. Or vice versa. As long as you are talking about things.

To some people, arguing is a way to deal with a difficult subject. I don't know why people think arguing isn't healthy. Maybe because what most people hope for is harmony without trauma.

CHAPTER EIGHT

Red Flags

Some people just love ignoring the big red flags. It's called denial.

When you see a giant red flag waving in your face, it is trying to say something to you. Usually it's saying, "This is not the right thing to be doing," or "There's something wrong with this picture." So when you see that red flag, pay attention to it. You know what a red flag is for.

You would pay attention to it at work.

You would pay attention to it with your brothers and sisters and your mother and father.

You would pay attention to it with your children.

Yet somehow we do not pay attention to red flags when it comes to our own relationships, and that's why I think there are so many divorces, because we all think,

WHOOPI GOLDBERG

"Oh, no, we can make it better." Let me tell you something: you can't.

Now, why do I say that?

When you talk to someone whose relationship has tanked, and you say, "Boy, how come you didn't see this coming? *We* all saw the red flags, and we know you saw the red flags. Those flags were gigantic." Your friend or your sister or whoever you're talking to doesn't know what to say because she made a decision that she was going to try to fix whatever was wrong with the relationship. Or, worse, she was ignoring it.

The thing is you can't make decisions for anybody else. You can't make someone do something she doesn't want to do. You can't do it. All you can do is put yourself where *you* want to be and work from that. If you happen to be lucky enough to find a like-minded person, all the better.

I have always thought it was just a little bit crazy that no one ever says, "If you're going to get married, you have to commit to the truth first." Wishful thinking is not a good strategy for a happy marriage. What I mean by this is if you're going to get into a relationship that leads to marriage, you have to be up front, first and foremost.

What does that mean? It means that once you know your own truth, you have to be clear to other people about who you are.

102

It means if you want to have kids, you need to get into that conversation early on.

It means if your career is always going to be your priority, you should explain that.

You need to say from the beginning, "Hey, this is who I am and this is what I do and I'm probably not going to change." Because finding things out down the road isn't a good thing.

Remember that you have the choice to see things as they are and not as you want them to be. Forgetting this is why I think so many people get divorced. When they got married, they knew who this person was. They may not have said it out loud, but inside, they knew. So then, five years down the line, when your husband or wife is still the person he or she was, you can't be shocked. You can't be angry. You knew what you were getting into and you got into it anyway. You just made the decision to ignore it. You thought you could fix it or that you could somehow deal with it. But you couldn't.

Can people evolve and shift? I'd like to think they can. I'd like to say probably. I don't know if they really, really do, though. They may try to be better or *say* they will be better—they may have the best intentions of doing so.

This whole thing reminds me of the fable of the scorpion and the frog. That's the story where a scorpion asks a frog if he can carry him across a stream. The frog says sure. They're halfway across when the scorpion stings the frog, and the frog is shocked because he's getting paralyzed and they're both going to drown. So he asks the scorpion why in the world he would do that, and the scorpion responds, "It's my nature."

People are who they are.

We all think men are just looking to plug a hole, which of course they are, especially in their twenties. But girls also want to act like whores at times in their lives. Your twenties are the time for you to run around and find shit out. There is a lot more to each of us, though, man or woman, and none of us should be dealing with stereotypes, because then you are setting yourself up and it's going to create problems.

If you really don't trust the person you're with because you know he is always trolling, my question to you is "Why are you with him?" It always comes back to that. "Why are you there?"

On the other hand, what if *you're* the troll? What if you're the person? You just have to be honest about it and say, "This is me, this is what I do. I go looking for other people. You may not be enough. Do you still want to stay?" Then they are either in or they are out, and there are no misunderstandings.

You have to listen. People are saying things, and you can't be rearranging their words to be what you want them to be. Listen to what they are saying and take it as fact from them. Now, how they're feeling could change. But for now, take it as fact.

If someone says, "This is not what I want," believe him.

If you're getting married and the guy says, "Look, I don't want to have kids," trust him. He doesn't want to have kids and shouldn't have kids to try to save something, because that doesn't work, because then you're mad at the baby. What does the baby know? She is just lying there trying to speak English. She doesn't know, and she didn't ask to be put in the middle of this situation.

Oprah always says, "When people show you who they are, believe them."

I will add: believe them *the first time*. Although, it's not always easy for us to do that. It might take two, three, or fifty times. But the truth remains the truth.

Now, why do people ignore the warning signs? For all the reasons we talked about earlier.

"Oh, I don't want to be alone."

"I don't want people to think I don't have anybody."

"I'm afraid I'll get old and no one will be attracted to me anymore."

"My biological clock is ticking."

"I can't have dinner by myself anymore."

Yes, someone I know actually used that last one as an excuse as to why she had a boyfriend. She would say, "I just wanted somebody to have dinner with."

It's like, "That's it?"

"Yeah, because it's so uncomfortable to go out to dinner by yourself."

That's ridiculous. That is, to me, dangerous—and also terrible for the other person, who thinks he is actually charming you into believing he is the person for you. And then when he discovers, "Ah, no, I'm not the man of her dreams. She just didn't want to eat out by herself." It's kind of a shitty position to put somebody in.

A lot of the time, not being up front about who you are starts at the very beginning, before there even is a relationship. It's why people lie in their online profiles. That's why they have that show on MTV, *Catfish*, where the guy goes and finds out who a person really is behind his or her online persona.

I can understand why people pretend to be other people online. I get that. In your online profile, you can be a better version of yourself, or a different you altogether.

You can be beautiful.

You can be skinny.

You can be white.

You can be black.

You can be Asian.

It's an avatar kind of world, so you can be whatever you want. But once you get busted in that lie, it's very hard to make a comeback, especially in a relationship.

Some people say, "Well, he wasn't exactly what I was

looking for, but I can mold him." Or "She wasn't exactly my first choice. She is not as pretty as I want her to be, but I can live with that." Those are two kind of terrible things to say about a person. You can't just say, "Oh, well, I'll live with it." Why would you want to? How is that going to end up? With both of you being happy? Why would you want to be with someone if you weren't his first choice? If he doesn't find you attractive or wants to mold you? It's insulting. I don't understand the point of that.

If you are never, ever, ever, not ever going to meet the person on the other side of that computer, sure, lie your pants off. Lie your pants off. If there is *no chance* you are ever going to meet—though you should know that in order to become a couple, you kind of have to meet—but if your avatars are meeting and that's all it's going to be, lie your pants off and have a good time, as long as you are both on the same page.

It's almost like playing a video game, like *The Sims*, where you can create your own world. If there is any possibility that you might want to meet this person, or that the other person might want to meet you, I would stay in the truth pool. Getting in the bullshittian pool is no good.

Beyond not being honest about who you are when you first meet someone, some people believe it's okay to tell little lies here and there in a relationship. I'm not a believer in that philosophy, whether you're lying about how someone looks or you're lying about what you are going through.

Like "I'm married."

Or "I'm separated but really want to get back together with my wife once you and I have this fling."

Or "I have an addiction problem."

Or "I used to be a call girl."

Or "I'm six figures in debt."

Or "I just lost my job."

Or "I have an eating disorder."

Or "I like to gamble—a lot."

Or "I like to shop—a lot."

Now, those are all big things to lie about, but there are also the little lies we tell, day to day, the ones that chip away at trust. These little lies are the ones that create doubt once someone catches on to them. These lies may seem harmless at the time you are telling them, but they do add up over time.

Like "I'm leaving the office now and will be home in time for dinner," when you know damn well you are going to the bar to have a few drinks with your colleagues.

Or "I'm just going to have one more and then we can go home."

Or "I will take your car to be serviced next weekend if I can play golf this weekend."

These may seem harmless, but when you don't deliver, when you tell these little lies, you are creating disappointment, and over time that disappointment will pile up. And you will be called unreliable.

If you tell a little lie in a relationship, even if it's an irrelevant one, and you get caught, you are always going to be the person who isn't totally trustworthy. You've created a little seed of doubt in your relationship.

There are stupid lies, too, like the ones that make the other person feel better. Say he asks, "Do these pants make me look big?" Well, you and I both know the answer is "Yes, those pants make you look big, and not only do they make you look big, but they are not flattering on you. I'm your partner. Why wouldn't you want me to tell you that truth? What would you want me to tell you? 'No, those are fine,' when I know they are not."

In other words, if you can't depend on me for the little shit, how can you be sure that you can depend on me for the big shit? If I'm willing to lie to you just to make you feel better, that's not being a good partner. That's someone who just is trying to keep the peace, and in a relationship, you shouldn't try to keep the peace.

I should be able to say, "Do not put those on. Don't put those on because they are not flattering" or "They don't make you look as good as you could be looking." Not in a mean way, but in a nice way. That's my job, to tell you the truth.

If your partner comes in and says, "I don't think you should wear that, I can see through it," or "You're really too big for this outfit," or "You're seventy-five years old and you're trying to dress like a fourteen-year-old," he is doing the right thing. That's important information for men and for women.

So if your wife says, "You cannot wear that because it doesn't look good," you need to hear it. You need to be able to accept that because that's a truth, and it's coming from the person who lives with you, who knows what looks good on you, or feels he knows.

Now, remember, you're only saying this if someone says to you, "Do I look fat in this?" If your husband or wife or partner comes in and, out of the blue, says, "That doesn't look good on you," that's a different thing, when the opinion is unsolicited, and you haven't asked him to give you any feedback.

However, you want him to take a chance and say to you, "Hey, I love you. I don't think you should wear that." That's okay, because if you are both complete people, then you will recognize that the other person is trying to do you a favor and keep you from being embarrassed. You recognize it because you're not looking to him to complete you or to do any of that shit. But you are looking to each other to tell the truth. And if the truth is "That suit is too small for you," or "Nobody wants to see your bread basket"—you know what I'm talking about, gentlemen; it's the male equivalent of camel toe—"and now I know you're Jewish. I didn't think you were, but because your pants are so tight, it has now been confirmed." If all that comes from someone who actually gives a shit about you, it's okay. It's better, it's honest, and it's real. You might not want to hear it. But then you can't bitch when you go out and you hear somebody whisper, "Oh, my God, why is she wearing that?" or "Why is he wearing that. That looks ridiculous on him!" after your partner has tried to tell you don't come out looking like that, and you were just halumphing him. Don't do it.

You don't want to hurt people's feelings for no reason, so you want to be cognizant of how you say things to them. You don't want to be an asshole. So be clear about what you're going to say and how you say it. And be kind. If I can't trust you as the one person in my life I'm supposed to be able to trust, how do you build a relationship from there? So, to me, without that first truth, without that absolute first truth, it's very tricky for people, and thinking that you're going to be able to change it later is a huge mistake.

There are ways to be kind and thoughtful and still get your point across. There's a way to disagree with someone and still treat him or her with respect. Don't "go along just to get along." Don't belittle or dismiss someone because he has a different point of view from you. There's a way to share your truth without being aggressive or defensive. And there is a way to listen to someone else's truth without getting hurt or angry.

Now, going back to what I said earlier, if I'm a player, before we go any further in this relationship, I need to let you know that, because you need to be able to make the decision whether to stay with me. That should be your decision. I already have my information. This is who I am. This is what I'm going to do. So you, on the other side, should have the opportunity to say, "My line in the sand is I don't want to be with the player. As much as I think you are fantastic and could bone you every day, I'm not going to be in a relationship with you because eventually your being a player is going to make me unhappy, and then we will both be miserable. So let's nip this in the bud." Those truths are important.

I've said it before and you will hear me say it again and again, because I feel like people need to hear it: Don't think you can change this just because you want it to be different. Know what your line in the sand is. If that's your line, then say, "I can't go past that."

If you're with a person who you know has other people in his life, committing to him might not be the smartest idea. And I'm not just talking about a married person. In the neighborhood, they would say if he's a player or she's a player, chances are she's always been a player and she's always going to be a player.

112

Now, the only thing you have to decide is are you okay with that? If you are okay with him being a player, then proceed. If you're not, do not go down the path. You're not going to change his behavior. It might stop for a little while, but it's not going to change. So the decision you make is your education. "Yes, I know this person fools around, but I'm okay with it because it's not the thing that motivates me. I'm all right with it."

While I haven't met a lot of people who are okay with that, there are also not that many people who will say, "Hey, I don't want to be with someone who is sleeping with fifty people." Instead, people say, "No, no, I'm going to do this anyway because I know I can change him."

I am telling you: you can't change him. And you can't be pissed off that's who he is, because you knew it before. You went into it knowing. You see these things. You feel these things. Your instincts tell you everything you need to know—"Danger, Will Robinson!"—because your stomach turns over, or somebody says something to you and it's just got that little tone and it's like…"Hmmm, is something going on?" Then you hear it again. And you say to yourself, "No, no, that can't be happening. I'm imagining it." So you are in denial or you ignore it or you think you can fix it later, and so you say, "Yes, I'll marry you." Like, wait. No, no, no. That's not going to work. It might work for a little while, but eventually the shit will hit the fan.

You've got to talk about this. Those are the red flags. Those are the red flags, and your body knows them. Everybody knows that clenching sensation in the stomach when you feel something that says, "I don't like this. This is not good behavior." Yet we go forward and invest in the relationship anyway. We do it for all the reasons that I've been talking about. We want to have that magical "happily ever after." How do we know who lived happily ever after? They just say it at the end of the story. But who actually did it? Has anyone? Cinderella? I don't know. How did her kids turn out?

As the song goes, players gonna play. If you're with a player, he is going to play. He is just going to do that. Cheaters are going to cheat. They're scorpions, right? They can't help it. They are not people who are comfortable with just one person. They've learned how to lie and make you feel like you are imagining things. They will say, "No, it's you. You don't trust me. I'm not doing anything." But it ain't you. You should have the right to know that up front, because otherwise it can do your head in.

If it turns out that there were no signs, and you never saw anything, and no one ever said to you, "Hey, it's kind of weird what I see going on in your relationship," and you really believe that your player boyfriend isn't playing, if none of that happened, then this book may have led you down the wrong path.

I think you do see signs, though, and I think people tell you things. Whether they say it out loud to your face or you just feel it in your gut, you know when something is being said. Living in denial isn't going to help anything, and a player isn't going to change his stripes.

Just an aside: people will see shit in your relationship that they don't see in their own. Do you care what your friends think? Do you listen to them when they say, "He is a dirty dog," or "She's really kind of loose and you don't want that"? Or do you do, as some of my friends have done, banish people, never to speak to them again until there's a divorce, and then say to everybody, "Oh, I should have listened to you."

Why put yourself through this?

True, people ignore their own issues but are very aware of the issues in your life. Just be aware of that. Sometimes people are telling you things to mess you up, or hurt you, or put you in a trick bag, but 80 percent of the time, you know what's going on, whether you want to admit it or not.

If your man was fucking around when you met him, he will be fucking around after you marry him. If you're cool with that, fantastic. You don't have anything to worry about, because you won't be running to divorce court. You can say, "I accept that. I can do that. That's cool." Because everybody knows what they've got as soon as they've walked into it.

I have an issue when people don't know that the person they are with—wait, what I mean is not that they don't know, but that they *don't acknowledge to themselves* that there is something going on here. If you don't have any reason to be hiding stuff, then, sure, why shouldn't your partner have your password? Because, you know, eventually you are going to call and say, "Oh, my God, I'm trying to get into my e-mail and I can't remember my password." Now, if you have been bullshitting about what your password is, then you have a little issue on your hands. So, for me, if you don't have any reason to hide stuff from your partner, why do it and create this hazard that doesn't need to be there?

Now, maybe you say to your partner, "You know what? I just feel like that's my private stuff, and I can say what I want and I can be the person I want to be." Your partner has every right to respond, "Are you saying it to anybody else?"

Because, see, when you put doubt in the relationship, when you give somebody a reason to wonder if something is happening on the side, that's not good. That also leads to divorce. If you're a person who is in a relationship, or you are going to get married, you need to tell the person you're with, "Hey, I made a friend. I made a new friend, and it feels odd, because it feels like I'm getting a tug, I'm getting a release." Whether it is an ego boost or a sexual release or attraction, it doesn't matter. A secret release is a relationship. Sorry. If you meet somebody online, and you're already married, and you're sharing with him and giving to him, that's a relationship. That's cheating. Sorry. It doesn't feel like cheating because it's not physical, but you're cheating.

As I said, there are big lies and small lies. Technically, I'm not a fan of lies, but there are okay lies. There are lies your kids are going to tell you: "Did you burn that?" "No."

But if you left a mess in the kitchen, you have to fess up, especially if you're the only one in the house. If you're the only person who could have left the mess, you should probably say, "Yeah, I messed it up."

"Did you take out the garbage?"

"Yes, I did"—and you know you didn't? Now, do you really want the wrath of the other person who has asked you to do this? Do you want her wrath by lying to her and saying you did it when you didn't?

No, I can't think of a great reason to lie—unless you don't want to be on the phone with somebody. Or if you're home and you don't want to talk. Yeah, that's me. Sometimes people call, and I'll say in a whispery voice, "Tell them I'm not here." That is a lie. Now, that's a lie I can live with, but I'm not in a relationship. I'm not lying to my partner, understand?

Have I ever lied in a relationship? The fact that I got married as often as I did is a lie. I said it earlier in the book, I knew better and I hurt people because I should have said, "This isn't for me." So, yes, I have. And that's why I can say to you you're better off with the truth.

The other thing about lies is you have to keep track of them, and it's hard. The older you get, the harder it is, because you can barely remember where you put your keys, your glasses, and your underwear.

That's what happens when you leave your underwear somewhere and you go home, you change into your clothes and your partner goes, "Where are your underwear?" Now, you can lie and say, "Well, I pooped my pants and I had to take them off."

But then that person is going to wonder, "Well, why did you poop your pants? Are you okay? Should we go to the hospital? Oh, my God, are you dying?"

Just don't.

What, this has never happened to you?

So, if you can help it, don't lie. The sun is brighter, your life is better, and everything is easier and simpler.

CHAPTER NINE

You Either Have "It" or You Don't

There are some people in the world who just have "It." And they are always going to get some, because they just can. It is charisma, sensuality, and sexuality all rolled into one. It oozes. Think of Marilyn Monroe. She just had It. Gay men, straight men, gay women, straight women—everyone wanted to touch her, and you can't explain why. You just knew that you must touch her. She was like velvet. You know how you feel about velvet. You just want to roll up on her.

I've only felt that way about the minions. You know,

the little yellow guys from *Despicable Me*. I don't know why, but I just wanted to touch them and kiss them on the head.

It is just an energy that other people want to be close to; it makes them tingly. It's attraction, but to the umpteenth degree. The best example of It I can give you is Jean-Paul Belmondo, the French movie star. One day, I was in a restaurant. I looked out the window and everything stopped, the air became very still. There was nothing else happening because I had just spotted Jean-Paul Belmondo. Let's just say I was breathless. (That's the title of one of his movies, by the way.) He had to be eighty-one at the time. When I tell you it was all I could do to keep my knees together, to keep my legs from flying open, and to keep myself from saying, "Entrez-vous." All I can say is, he had It. It was oozing out of him, into the restaurant, up my chair, in my face, kind of going, "Hey!" and every fantasy imaginable ran through my head. The man was eighty-one. And I know that if we'd have done the deed, he would have killed me before I killed him. Given all I know about the world, while he may not have approached me for a relationship, we could have arranged a booty call. And there's nothing wrong with a booty call, because sometimes you just want to hit it and run. Especially if it's Jean-Paul Belmondo.

Yeah, I would have given Jean-Paul Belmondo a booty call, y'all.

For some reason, people think this is a bad thing. I don't. Booty calls can keep you from making strategic mistakes. If you're in a sexual place and you have a friend who doesn't want any more from you than that and your friendship, I say go to him. As long as you both have the same expectations and articulate them so you understand one another.

Which brings me to this: If you're with a man or woman who has It or you're a person who has It, and you know you have It, and you meet somebody and you say, "Hi, I'm going to partner up with you," you need to let him know this is who you are. You need to let him know that this your way, meaning you are a sexy beast and people are going to be drawn to you.

It sort of goes back to being with a player. While people who have It may not necessarily be players, it does mean that other people are constantly going to be attracted to them, to want them. If you are with this person, you may find that threatening or even annoying. If you meet somebody who has It, really pay attention and see how people respond to him.

I know a couple, and the man has It. There's no question. She, after meeting him and realizing that she kind of dug him, started to just watch interactions he had with other people and how other people responded. Based on that, she made her decision about whether she could be with him as a partner.

When you're with someone who has It, the people around you will say they didn't notice, even if they did. Meaning, your girlfriends, acquaintances, the waitress, and anyone else in the vicinity has, or is going to, hit on your man. People will put it out there. So you have to develop some skills and be sharp and on top of your game.

That's why I say to pay attention to the way other people talk to you, and to consider what their agenda may be in telling you something. More often than not, they are telling you something because of their own issues. They are either trying to get to you. Or trying to get rid of you. Or they are boning your guy. Or trying really hard to. So recognize when someone is messing with you and be prepared to deal with it.

It is not an easy kind of relationship, being with someone with It, so you have to make a decision if you can live with someone who has It or not. Then you and the It person have to sit down and work out some parameters on behavior, out of respect for you. I know this only because I have been there and done that. But I'm not going to tell you which side I was on...

Not too long ago, I was at a function and saw a woman who looked sixty years old. She was a gorgeous lady, and somebody said, "You know she's eighty?" I said, "Who?" And this beautiful woman turned around and said, "Me."

I was like, "Oh, no." I couldn't believe this woman was eighty. I watched her in action, and it was impressive. There was no question this woman had It.

That's right. It has no expiration date. People who have It usually keep it for their entire lives. It's not about physical beauty or even just general sexiness. It's just an energy that attracts other people. When someone has It, it defies old age.

They're pretty lucky. For other people, shit is changing every day. They're afraid that they are going to get old and nobody is going to want them, so they look and behave younger than they ever have. They go to the gym, they stay active, they dye their hair, they get a little Botox.

Age can be a big thing with women. It drives fear, and that is utter bullshit. Women are afraid that once they get older, men will no longer find them attractive. That there's some sort of expiration date on them. This goes beyond the so-called biological clock. The truth of the matter is you never know who is going to find you attractive. You never know where chemistry is going to happen.

Women are as attractive as they want to be. Take this face, my face—it is not the face that launched a thousand ships; a thousand laughs, maybe, but not a thousand ships. I was never raised to think that it was about my face. It was always about my head, my brain. My mother was very clear with me about that from a young age—I was going to have to develop myself and use my intelligence to get whatever I wanted because the face wasn't going to do it.

So my brain is pretty good, and when I want to attract something or someone, when I'm ready, I just open it up. I open up my energy and put it out there. Then, when I'm done, I close it shut. I can put out the "come hither" finger. It's all about attitude. When I met that eighty-year-old woman, I saw her do it to a younger guy who was just like, "Wow, this woman is amazing," and then I saw her turn it off. It was the most remarkable thing. It made me think, "Maybe everybody can do that. If they're smart enough."

Attitude is important that way. When you're walking around with your head down or your eyes glued to your phone, this is not saying, "Come talk to me." If you're walking around with your head up, a smile on your face, and an open expression, with an energy, and then you zoom in on somebody, that's saying, "You know what? You might want to come and talk to me. I might have something interesting to say to you."

Think back to the older woman. She's standing there, thinking, "So, you think because I'm eighty that maybe I'm not all that interesting, maybe I'm not for you. First, come over and talk to me. You don't have to get past any preconceived notions yet. See what I have to say, what I have to offer. Now, you want to talk to me again?

Each time you come back, you might get a little bit more, unless I realize you're an asshole and then I'm gone again. I turn it off."

When people approach you, to talk to you, you know, you can control your attitude. Each of us can: men, women, little kids. Little kids are the best with it. When they want your attention, you are going to know, and they will jump through hoops and have no shame in getting you to pay attention. It's like these little arms going, "Hey! I'm here! Watch me! Listen to me!" It's a wonderful thing.

It's something you can do, too, in your own way, so be aware of it.

How Do You Start Dating Again After Fifty?

After fifty or sixty or whatever, the first thing to do is find yourself a cannon, aim it in the direction you want to go, and shoot yourself out of it.... What do you mean "How do you get back in the dating world after fifty?" How did you get into the dating world the first time? You met people, you went to bars, you went to dinner, you had friends who had other people, who maybe weren't hooked up with other folks—that's how you do it. And of course now there is a huge variety of dating websites to make it that much easier for you if you really have no friends or local bars.

You gotta get over this idea that after a certain age you're not supposed to be hooking up or looking for sex or a relation-ship or whatever. What is that? You can have as much sex as you want to have for as long as you want to have it. And when

126

you don't want to have it anymore, say, "It's not for me anymore."

Are you dating because you want to find somebody to spend your life with and you're looking for another relationship, another marriage perhaps? I don't know if that's the best thing for you. But if your religion says you shouldn't be out there without a partner, then you have to figure that out. Regardless, just do what we have done for centuries. We get our friends involved and we meet people who are interesting to us. Sometimes they're not exactly our same age. Sometimes you're a little younger; sometimes they're a little older. Or vice versa. And there are a lot of positive things that come with both directions, but you have to make a decision.

Do you want to get back out there? If you do, what are your expectations? You have to name what you want. Write it down. If you know what you want, and you're clear on it, then write it down and act accordingly.

Call your friends.

Call your kids, if you're lucky enough to have kids.

Call your brothers and sisters, if you have them.

If you're an only child, I'm hoping you have some friends.

Go hang out.

That's what you got to do. Then, if someone says, "Let's do this again," I believe that constitutes a date. You take me out more than once, I think it's a date, but you might not.

If you're looking for somebody to marry, that's a whole other thing, because you've got to get into the groove of people who are of your age group who are looking for that. Because, really, are you ready at sixty to have more kids? I don't think so. Are you ready at seventy, eighty? For guys, yes, that makes sense. For women, not so much, because we got one quarter of an egg holding on. Why even bring somebody into the world if you're sixty? Some people have done it. I think it's kind of crazy, but I'm not in their shoes.

So let's get back to this. Write down what you want. Talk to the people around you and don't listen to your kids when they tell you, "Don't do this." Do not listen to them. The fact of the matter is you're old enough to know whether you want to hang out or just have a hit-and-run every now and then. Your call.

CHAPTER TEN

Let's Talk About Sex

There has always been a difference between having sex just for the sake of sex versus having sex in a relationship. We all know that.

And then, of course, there is lust.

Most people don't pay attention to chemistry and the way it affects us. They are looking for something else. They are looking for somebody else. Often the people you have chemistry with are people you are trying to get away from because they don't fit your idea of what a relationship is supposed to be or your idea of the right person for you. When you find that chemistry, your body knows it. Your system kicks into gear, the blood starts to flow. You start to get flushed. Suddenly your tits are sitting up a little higher. That's chemistry. That's all the things chemistry does. It says we are connected somehow, and it isn't a rational thing.

We might be connected only for the evening. You wake up the next day and there's no chemistry left. Get out. Good-bye.

I myself am a hit-and-run artist. Hit-and-runs are great because you're not committed, but you get yourself taken care of. Guys have been doing it for years, going to brothels and all that. Most women don't think that way and can't even accept that.

What's funny to me about all this is that if you had sex with a guy back in the day when I was growing up, you were instantly thought of as being a ho. Instantly. God help you if you got pregnant. Forty years later, we are still in the same place.

Women have the same needs as men. They just do. So why do we pretend they don't?

You can go out and have fun with somebody, spend time with him, and you can have fun with that same person for the next five or six months, all without writing your names in a little heart on your notebook or saying, "I'm going to be Mrs. So and So."

You're allowed to have fun and enjoy people for the time that is appropriate or that works for both of you, without having every relationship become a potential marriage proposal. Yet most of the books out there are still telling women that they shouldn't be having sex until date number three, and that if they want the man to be interested in them, they need to play hard to get. Why is this? Why are we constantly telling women that they have to "snag" a man and hold out on him with the whole goal being a marriage proposal?

This all just ignores chemistry.

Also, people should not be looking outside their own ideas of whom they should be looking for and whom they should be attracted to. Everybody thinks they should want someone who will be visually pleasing to other people. Women find themselves thinking, "Oh, I can't go off with him, because he isn't what other people want for me." So they miss a lot of stuff. But what's wrong with a little sense of adventure? You never know what you might learn about yourself.

So, yes, there is lust. You have chemistry in lust, and with lust, you can have sex with everybody. You can have chemistry with anybody. "Fire hydrant, I have lust for you. I'm going to have sex with you." It might just be "Hmmm, I feel a little horny today. I think I'm going to go out to the bar." Or "Oh, I met this guy, he's really nice. I'm just going to hit this right quick in the bathroom." Boom. Boom. Boom. Boom. Nobody the wiser. You're smart enough to take a condom with you. Keep it to yourself, so no one calls you a ho. What if you call yourself a ho? Well, you're being self-indulgent.

Most women have been taught, or have been given

WHOOPI GOLDBERG

this overwhelming feeling, that sex without a relationship is a bad thing. I'm not a believer in that. I don't want
a relationship, yet occasionally I want a little sex. I have
enough friends, so that if I make a call, one of them will
come over and say, boom, boom, good to see you. You
know, that's important. You have to give yourself that
ability to say, "I'm not looking for a relationship. I'm
looking to get laid."

Women don't do this nearly enough, and we're not
trained to do it. You know, for eons men have brought
their sons to brothels and said, "This is how you do this,
my son." But that's never been done with women. The
conversation has never even been had.

So I want to start the conversation. Let's ask the question what's wrong with it? Is it a moral issue? If it's a
moral issue for you, then you won't do it. Is it a religious
issue? Have you been raised to think that sex is bad, that
nice girls don't do it, that it goes against God's plan? Why
would the pleasure of sex exist if there were something
unnatural or something wrong with it?

If you just want to get laid and you're not looking to
marry this guy, what's wrong with that? I'll tell you what,
it's a double standard. A huge double standard. It's okay
for guys to do this but it's not okay for women? Why is
that? It hard to understand why this way of thinking still
exists and is so deeply ingrained in us.

Forty years ago I grew up with this double standard,

134

and here we are, forty years later, when women have gone through so much transformation—the invention of the Pill, the ability for women to earn their own money and have their own careers and independence, and the feminist movement—and yet somehow this hasn't been fixed. It was supposed to be fixed, and yet it wasn't. Somehow we've gone backward.

It's the same way for gay folks. Even folks who are into ducks. We're still hung up on sex.

Now, I'm not saying be reckless or stupid. I'm not saying to put yourself in any danger. Don't go looking for Mr. Goodbar. And use protection. Here is the thing: Any woman or any man, anyone, who has unprotected sex in this day and age has an altogether different agenda than just getting laid.

If you're going for a hit-and-run and you're not protecting yourself, what is that? It borders on self-destruction. Because this is a different world today than the world I grew up in. This is a world where you can catch stuff that will kill you. I have seen too many people die of AIDS. People I loved, people very close to me. And it is miserable. If you're having unprotected sex with somebody you've met, it's because you either want to get pregnant, you want to ensnare someone. Or you are in denial and being self-destructive. It's not a good thing.

Women have to learn to protect themselves. You cannot wait for the other person to pull out the condom.

You've got to pull the condom out and insist on it, and if there's a no in there, then you can't have a hit-and-run with that guy.

It is just common sense. No glove, no love.

People also get very upset when I suggest that sometimes you just need to go to, you know, the ladies who work—I don't call them ladies of the night, because they don't always work at night—women whose services you pay for. Sometimes, in a relationship, people can't always get what they need, and if you have reputable people you can turn to in order to get what you need, I say go for it. It is a whole lot better than being frustrated and angry at the person you love.

I know more couples who have that kind of relationship, and each person understands where the partner is coming from, and they've been together forever. Because maybe, just maybe, he doesn't want to spin on his head attached to the ceiling, and you do. Maybe she doesn't really want to have fifteen people with you in the bed. Maybe you just need to go get something different. And I say if you pay for it, make your partner aware of it and explain why, so she knows it has nothing to do with her, but just with what your particular needs may be. It's a fair way to approach it. Of course, this holds only if the service woman is clean, and you practice safe sex—that's why I say "reputable." Or be with someone you've had this kind of relationship with for a long time. If it's discussed and not just gone and done, it's best, because there are some things you're just not interested in doing, and some things the other person is into. That's okay. Rather than destroy an entire relationship because something sexual doesn't work, let's try to work it out.

People have to come to terms with the fact that the religious idea of "coupling" is not everyone's idea of coupling. Many religions tell us, at least they did in the old days, that if you got married, you had to stay married. You couldn't even get a divorce. Women couldn't ask for a divorce, which still happens today in a lot of third-world countries, where women are trapped in miserable or abusive marriages for life. So if you are stuck because of religious reasons, you have to try to work out something if you are going to stay in your marriage and be somewhat happy.

If religion guides your life, then you'd better know what's in the good book. Don't cast stones. Don't live in glass houses unless you're ready to get hit with those stones, and have your house come tumbling down on you. Don't judge. You're not God.

Depending on what your religion is, if you don't want to support the ideas I am writing here, that's all fine. I don't mind that you feel that way. You can like the book or not like the book. I didn't tell you to buy it, so don't you tell anybody not to buy it. I'm giving you what you want, which is the freedom to believe how you believe.

But don't step on me. You have your beliefs and I have mine.

The same thinking applies to your relationships. If you're ready to start up a relationship with somebody, talk about this kind of stuff up front. You'd better know where you guys stand with each other. He may be pro-choice, and she's not. You need to know that if you're a Christian pastor, you can't be sneaking around because, remember, just like you tell me God can see me, he can see you more, because you supposedly have a big aura around you. Be careful. Be very careful.

So talk to each other. Be open about where you stand and what you believe, so you're not sneaking around.

Love and sex. They are different things to different people, and both of them are loaded. They can mess you up. Sex in particular can really mess up your independence. It can put a damper on your self-love—and I don't mean masturbation; I mean love of self—because suddenly now you're dependent on a person who wants to have sex with you telling you you're okay. In any long-term relationship that's going to change. It's going to change whether you're a man or a woman. If you're a woman, you get to be a certain age, shit dries up. It just does. Changes happen, shit falls, shit spreads. Men, the equipment doesn't always work. Which means people beat themselves up when their sex lives aren't what they imagined them to be.

There are people that can be together for twenty years, and they are in sexless relationships, but they definitely have love. I see this all the time. A lot of the time, people misinterpret the sex for the love. People will say, "They are not having sex, so they can't be in love." But that's not necessarily true; it's just a different love, a deep friendship and companionship, a feeling of being family. The roots between sex and love are deep, so it depends on each individual's needs and making sure everyone's needs are being met one way or another.

Some guys don't want to sleep with their partner all the time. It's like, "No, can we just raise the kid? Can we just do this? I don't want to have sex with you." Or the wife loses interest in sex and tells the husband, "Go get a girlfriend. I'm not interested in sex anymore. Leave me alone." They don't want to get a divorce because they still love each other, they are best friends, and they are a family. They are good together in most ways. But they just don't want to have sex with each other anymore.

For some folks, it works out really well, but that's only when they are being honest. Since most people aren't honest about it, there is frustration and anger and a sense of betrayal. People have affairs, and then there is a lot of hurt. But if you're not having sex with each other, does that mean you shouldn't be allowed to have sex at all? You've got to talk about it and come up with a solution that works for both of you.

Now, some people are just martyrs, but 90 percent of those people say, "It's me, isn't it? You don't have any love for me anymore. You're not attracted to me anymore." That is the worst possible thing you can do. Your mate, if he or she is not fooling around behind your back, may be going through the Change—I'm talking about menopause or man-o-pause again, people—it has nothing to do with you. That's physiological. That's the stuff that really is happening. Your body is saying, "Hey, I don't need to do this anymore because I'm not having any more kids" so things shift. But baby, that green-eyed monster is pretty awful. It's pretty awful. She comes up out of the blue, which would make her the blue-green-eyed monster, but it's better to treat each other like friends and not let the blue-green-eyed monster mess things up for you.

I have a friend whose wife didn't have sex with him for three years, and it wasn't his choice. He kept trying, and eventually he got tired of getting rejected and found a side piece. When the wife eventually found out, she went ballistic. She called him a sexual deviant. She made him go to a shrink to discuss his deviancy, and in order to save his marriage, he went along with it. He went to the shrink, he apologized to her, but at no point did he say, "Whoa, you rejected me for three years and that doesn't work for me. What's going on here? Let's talk about it and figure it out together." Unless the wife engaged in this conversation with him, it would be just a matter of time before he either went back to the side piece or found a new one. (By the way, if she thinks he is a deviant, I can only imagine what she will think about me after she reads this book.)

The thing about sex is that, again, because nobody really talks about it, we're taught that once people get married they are having it and it lasts forever. Well, it's only in the last twenty years anyone has started talking about things like erectile dysfunction or menopause, or the changes that your body goes through as you get older. Yes, these things have always existed, but they weren't openly discussed. That's why the old folks always say that after the sex is gone, that's when you find out where you stand with the other person. If there was nothing there but the sex, and you can't connect without the sex, make the booty call and find that thing that fulfills you. Or that person who fulfills you.

A question I get asked a lot is "What is it about marriage that can kill sex?" My answer is sex dies for lots of reasons. There is an emotional piece and there is a physical piece.

On the emotional side, marriages can turn into business arrangements, or friendships, or companionship, and the sex fades away. I often hear from women that they get mad at the man for whatever reason; he did something they didn't like and so they hold a grudge and they withhold sex. They get resentful, or they have babies. The men always complain, "You had a baby and now you love the baby more than you love me." You're like, "Yes, that's true."

Or the man loses his job and the woman gets pissed off. So she thinks, "I'm mad at you, so I'm not having sex with you." Sometimes it's not necessarily conscious, it just happens.

Or they spend the time talking about paying the bills or who is taking the kids to school, all that mundane stuff that makes up a marriage, and the sex gets lost.

Or everyone is just exhausted. There are so many things that married people have to do that prevent them from spending days in bed together.

That is different than when sex dies because your vagina changes or somebody's penis changes. Sex is killed when you can't do it anymore because it doesn't work the way you want it to. Sometimes, for the woman, it just hurts. And for the man, he can't get it up anymore. These things can happen with age. If you know you're going through the Change, tell your partner so that he can understand what's happening so that he can go through it with you. You can find different ways to enjoy one another.

Oftentimes the partner's affection for the other person doesn't go. Sometimes it's just that you don't want to climb on somebody. You're just not in the mood, but it doesn't mean you wouldn't go for a little cuddling. Any kind of affection is sex to me, and all affection is sex once you're married.

So if you're in communication with each other and things are changing, or your body is changing, or you feel different, you should be able to work through this with the person you're with and say, "Here is what's happening to me," and not be afraid he is never going to talk to you or never going to want you again. You have to put it on the table.

It seems like a lot of marriages break up when one of the partners is around fifty. Well, forty-five to fifty-five. And a lot of the time I think it's because of menopause or perimenopause. The woman's testosterone goes higher, and the man's estrogen goes higher. There is this shift. It's like being a teenager again, but instead of increasing your sex drive, it messes it up. Shit changes, but nobody talks about it.

Again, speak up. Women need to say, "Here are the issues I think are going to be in my life because I am changing. So you should know it has nothing to do with me not wanting to be with you, but there are physical things that are happening." And then you do what you can to keep it going. But you also have to be honest and say, "I don't feel like I want to do it as often as I used to." People don't have these conversations enough, but they are important. If you're not talking, then everything comes as a surprise and bad feelings come up.

Men also need to step up and say, "I don't know; it doesn't get hard the way it used to. I don't know what's happening." Men often worry that this makes them less of a man. But it doesn't, it just means something is going on. If you can't tell your partner something is going on, then what's the point of being with her?

With men, sometimes it's the prostate as they get older, and sometimes it's just a drop in testosterone. People don't talk about men's hormones, but they do exist. You want to get to a point in your relationship where the guy can say, "This is what's going on. Let's go to the doctor and figure this out. Because I want to do it, but I just can't seem to get it up. It has nothing to do with you, but I am frustrated."

As I've said, all this communication with your partner is really important because it gives you insight. You have to allow yourself to hear what's happening without making it about you, because it's not always about you—usually it's not about you at all. If you can have the conversation, you're ahead of the game, because you find ways to compensate. You can say, "Okay, so we're not able to play stick-in-the-donut. But we can, you know, rub up against each other in the elevator when nobody is looking." There are things you can do to continue that part of life and enjoy it. It's not just about getting on top of somebody. It's about the emotional connection that you have, and figuring out how the two of you are going to physically connect. There are lots of ways to do it. You have to be intelligent and straight about it.

Men can take Viagra. For women it's not as easy. The FDA recently approved a new drug that people are calling women's Viagra. But the thing is, it doesn't make you want to have sex; it only makes you moist. So supposedly it makes it easier to have sex. But there are side effects, and it's a pill you have to take every day. So the jury is still out.

Then there's lube, but you have to be careful with that stuff. Some of it can be toxic, and some people's bodies can't take it. You have to really try to figure it out together. I have a friend who tried some lube, and she got the biggest rash. Somehow it triggered a reaction with the guy, and he passed it on to her. She also did some research and told me the stuff they use to lube condoms has Nonoxynol-9 in it, which is what they used to use in World War II to clean airplanes. It's like Coca-Cola: it will take the rust off a car. Why are you putting that there? If you don't know what's in this stuff, it can hurt you, so you have to educate yourself, do your research, and figure it out together. There's no one answer for everyone.

CHAPTER ELEVEN

Not Everyone Wants to F*** You

One question I hear from time to time is "How do you know when to pursue sex with somebody?" I don't think they're asking about the "don't have sex until the third date" rule. I think they're asking, "How do you know if you want to have a sexual relationship with someone?" Some people might say, "Isn't it obvious?" No, not always. We're human, so like everything else we've talked about, there's no one easy answer.

We know from these long-term marriages that there can be strong love without sex. We also know it from how we interact with people every day. Listen, I have loved so many men whom I've had no desire to have sex with. If I were to have sex with them, it would change everything. It's not money that changes everything, Cyndi Lauper, it's sex.

Sex changes everything.

Sex makes people nuts.

Sex makes people possessive.

Sex makes people boastful.

Sex makes people lie.

Sex makes people turn into assholes and bitches.

Because, for some reason, as we talked about earlier, the mythology of a relationship says that sex lasts with one person and one person only, and it lasts forever, and that you should not want any deviation from that. You're not supposed to see anyone else as a sexual being. You're not supposed to have lustful thoughts in your heart. It's terrible. Sexual desire becomes like a jail. I base my opinion here on my own relationships. I have been there and done that.

I'm a really sexual person. I really, really am. I'm not so much now, because I've come into my own, and I realize what's right for me. Still, I have not avoided booty calls when they have presented themselves, and I've made a phone call or two here and there. In my experience, though, sex makes people nuts. There are so many beautiful people in the world that sometimes you look over at someone and he just gives you a little tingle, like Tinker Bell.

If you admit this, people immediately get very uptight with you.

"Why do you have that smile on your face?"

"What are you looking at?"

"What are you doing?"

It's like, "Whoa, whoa, whoa, he's hot. I just got a little moist. It doesn't mean I'm not moist for you."

Somehow, when you're in a relationship—even if it's the beginning—and it looks like you're going to become sexual partners, you need to discuss how it relates to the other people in your life. A little while ago on *The View* we talked about the idea of not being able to have friends of the opposite sex, which I think is insane. Somebody who was recently on the show said, "You know, my husband gets so nervous whenever I'm around other men. He doesn't realize I'm looking at him with everything that we've always had, but there are beautiful people in the world, and I can't get him to understand that it's not a threat."

This ridiculousness of men and women not being able to be friends boggles my mind. I have so many friends who say, "If my partner speaks to a girl, or has girlfriends, I don't like that; I should be enough." Or guys will say, "She has too many male friends. I don't like that; I should

be enough." Well, you're not. People need to have friends.
Men need to have women friends, if only to teach them
that not every woman is a sex object for them. Men
have to know how to be friends with women. Women
have to know how to be friends with men. Not just gay
men, ladies. You have to know how to be friends with
hot, gorgeous men so you can secretly say to yourself,
"Boy, I would gnaw on that leg if I had a hot minute,
but that's not what we are. That's not what our friendship is." You must be able to have that. Men and women
have a lot to learn from one another, and being friends
is a great way to do it.

Now some people might say, "You don't think that
with men and women, even in friendships, that sex is
hanging over them at all times? Isn't there this potential thing that is going to get in the way? And even if
you are not attracted to someone aren't men just dogs
who are always going to try?" I can tell you that I have
male friends that I would never, ever consider having sex
with. Let's put it this way: let's liken straight men and
women being friends to gay people being friends with
other gay people of the same sex. If sex and attraction
were always hanging over every friendship, then every
lesbian couldn't have female friends and every gay guy
could never have guy friends—which is ridiculous.

That comparison alone takes the teeth out of the
bullshit of that argument. What's really going on is that

most people don't trust their mates. That's the problem. If you don't trust the person you're with, there are bigger issues there. Much bigger issues.

If you are so paranoid and think that if he talks to another woman he is going to run off with her, there's something wrong, and you two should be talking about that. You should explain why this is a problem for you. Why is it that you can't let your guy talk to another woman? You think it's because all women are just waiting to steal your man? Or your guy won't let you talk to another guy because that kind of guy, he is just going to come and steal you and take you away? You can't have that shit.

It's one of the things that drives me crazy on the show. Women would say, "No, he can't have any women friends." And I would ask, "Well, what, you don't trust him?" They would say, "No, I don't trust *her.*" It's like, but that's your friend.

I find it extraordinary. With all my male friends, their wives and girlfriends know I'm their friend. I will call a male friend—I won't call at stupid hours, like you do when somebody is living by himself—but I'll call and see how he's doing, and all that stuff, and suggest we go out, and of course that he invite his old lady.

I have a friend who is one of the most beautiful men who I have ever seen who also wanted to be my friend. And I was like, "Really?" He was like, "Yeah." "Okay," I said. Then I met his old lady, who is equally beautiful, and she knows that he will go walking down the street and women will fall out of trees. They just fall right in front of him. She is totally aware that this happens. But she is not afraid, because she knows him. She knows that's he's not going to be catching all these women falling out of the trees. That's not who he is. That is her knowledge. That is her belief. He doesn't stray, and she doesn't sweat it at all. It is one of the best relationships I have ever seen.

Jealousy, that's the word. You cannot have jealousy present in the relationship. You can feel a little jealous sometimes. It happens. When you see somebody who is really hot standing a little too close to your partner, don't just stand there getting upset. Walk on over and stand next to them and smile and be part of the conversation until you get bored and walk away. Then your partner eventually comes to find you. If your partner doesn't come to find you, you have a problem. Unless the conversation was so good they just kept talking. It doesn't mean he is leaving you. It just means they had a great conversation. Did they exchange e-mails? It's possible. But you should be able to tell your partner, "She was quite interesting. She runs the UN." Or "He dives for pearls and is a philosophy major" without having them feel threatened. These are interesting people, but it doesn't mean you are interested in them sexually. It just means you're interested in them, and you should be interested in interesting people. That should not be something that you avoid because your partner is going to be jealous and think you are going to run off with one of them. That's not a good thing.

So, men and women, you can have a hot, young friend who doesn't have sex with you. It's okay. You can have a hot young friend. It's just the way it is.

Women, when you see a hot, young guy whom you like, who is interesting, and think, "If I weren't married and that person weren't married, and we were on Mars... well, who knows what would happen." Not a problem. You can have relationships and friendships—and I should make the distinction when I say "relationships." You can have friendships with people you are not involved with. You should be able to. Male or female. Gay or straight.

I have a good time with the people I love. The people I love are the people I love, and I am much better now with my relationships because I learned that I can like you or love you and not have sex with you. Great. And you get to stay my friend. How wonderful. This is important.

A lot of the times when women are good friends with a guy, when they have a connection, they come to the conclusion that sex is the next step. But it isn't always. A girlfriend of mine met a guy who loved the same old movies and indie films, so they started going to movies together. Then they would go sit in a café and talk and talk. They developed an amazing connection. She wasn't necessarily attracted to him physically, but she thought maybe they were in love and should have sex. So they did, and it was a disaster. It wasn't meant to be. Fortunately they were able to get over that and laugh about it and stay friends. They probably shouldn't have tried the sex to begin with, because why make a wonderful thing more complicated than it needs to be? They had a great connection, and she should have just been happy with that. That friendship has lasted longer than any of her lovers, by the way.

Sometimes we forget how to be friends, especially with the people who are also our lovers. We just don't communicate enough. You know how your personality is, so let me know that. If someone hurts your feelings, what's your response going to be? Are you a jealous person going in? Are you the type to think, "I suffer from jealousy and I don't want to see you looking at anybody else." I have to know that up front. And then I can decide, "Do I want to be with this person? Yes, it's worth it." Or "No, it's not."

If you can communicate about that, then you can communicate about other important things. You should be able to say, "Oh, I don't like that you said that. That really bothered me that you said that." Or "That really hurt my feelings." He should say, "I'm really sorry." That way these things get resolved up front and everyone knows where everyone else stands.

You should be open, be yourself, express your feelings and be friends. If you're friends with someone and he says something that hurts your feelings, you would be able to tell your friend. Why wouldn't you want that in a relationship, too?

What I'm hoping is that people will take a little more time to figure out if the person they are with is someone they want to be with. Not that they *need* to be with or they think they should be with. But that they actually *want* to be with. Is this somebody I will not mind hanging out in the park with? Can I walk down the street and hum with him? Can we have a good time together? Can I tell him the truth? Can I say, "This is what hurts me," or "This is what makes me happy." Can I say that to this person?

In a relationship, it's important to say these things about one another. It's crucial. You hear other people say mean stuff or hurtful stuff to one another and you think to yourself, "Why is he talking to her like that?" or "Why is she talking to him like that?" You know when the words being spoken between people aren't nice. When they are meant to hurt or are disrespectful or dismissive. When you hear it, you think, "We'll that's kind of shitty. That's not a healthy relationship." And you think, "If we were friends, would you be talking to me like that?" I think it's an important question. Are we friends? Are you going to talk to me like a friend? It's something people don't pay enough attention to.

I believe in soul mates, but I don't believe that you have to have sex with your soul mate or that you have to marry your soul mate. But let me ask you, what does that mean, to have a soul mate? It's a connection. And it can mean different things to different people. There isn't one hard and fast definition. And I think you can have a lot of soul mates; there isn't necessarily just one.

I have four soul mates right now. They are people for whom I would give my life. But I wouldn't have them come live with me in my house. I don't want to marry them. They are married to other people anyway, thank God, so they don't want that, either. Theirs are relationships that have endured many wives and husbands, and all those people came to terms with the fact that I'm here, and I'm friends with their spouses. Everybody involved knows I'm not going to run off with their husband. I'm not going to take. I'm not going to touch. But this person, your partner, has been my friend for a long time, longer than you've been together. You will have to deal with it. Periodically, I'm going to call. I will be respectful. That's what friends do.

So a soul mate is not necessarily a person who you would go run off with, or marry. It's just great to have someone who can talk to you without judgment, someone who cares about you and accepts you just the way you are.

The word *soul mate* means different things to different people. Besides, we connect with different people for different reasons. Only you will know what a soul mate feels like. You may have to cop to the fact that your soul mate doesn't look the way you think he should. So when you find him, you go, "Oh, my God. It's *you?*"

A lot of people think there is just one soul mate in the world for them and spend their lives looking for him or her. They think if they try hard enough, they will find "the one." They find someone they connect to and think, "You're my soul mate. Let's have sex and let's get married and be in love forever." But that isn't usually how it works.

You have to realize that everybody you come in contact with does not want to have sex with you. And if we're saying that one should really learn how to have friends that are not sexual, then stop with the sex. Learn how to just be a person to someone else. If you have dear friends, they are the people that make your soul whole.

When is it right for people to pursue sex? I guess whenever they are feeling mutually sexy toward one another. Don't take it personally if you feel it and he doesn't. It's not at all a rejection of you. It may not be what he wants from you. And you can't be mad at him because he doesn't want to bone you. If you think that way, then you are just downgrading yourself. There's more to you than your sex, and you should act and dress that way.

I had dinner with a girlfriend the other night in New York, where we film *The View*. She said, "Here all these guys want is 'this' "—and she pointed down to you know where—"They don't want anything else." I said, "You have to find a guy who is not from New York."

But the real question then becomes: Are you going to places that are known as pickup joints? If you're in a pickup joint, somebody is going to try to pick you up and try to have sex with you. Perhaps you need to reevaluate how you are spending your time. Perhaps you need to go bowling or volunteering instead.

If you go out and your chest is hanging out, or you're wearing very tight pants and you have a bulge in your pants, women are going to want to touch you. If you put yourself out as an object, people are going to treat you like an object. If you put yourself out as a person, 85 percent of the time they will treat you as a person. But you have to draw that line. You have to show people how to treat you. And I have said this before: you just have to be patient.

Now let's get to some more questions.

How Do You Get Past a Cheating Partner and Rebuild Trust?

Oftentimes, if your partner has cheated, it may be something he or she has done in the past. Maybe back then you kind of let it go, thinking that once he was with you everything was going to be okay and that he would stop. But you have to ask yourself, "Is this person just a serial cheater or is there something going on in our relationship that I'm not paying attention to that caused this?"

I don't know if you can actually rebuild trust in a year or two. It might take five years. Do you want to do the work? If you're willing to believe that this is not going to happen again, then you put your best foot forward. If you think it might happen again, then maybe you want to take a little separation time. What you don't want to do is say or give the vibe of "I know what you're

159

doing," and accuse him of still doing it when he is truly sorry and trying not to. If in fact he has stopped doing it, and then you drive him to do it again because now you've made him the bad guy while you're the mensch who took him back—well, no one wants to have to have that hanging over his head or live with a victim. If you're giving him another chance, you have to let it go and trust him—if that's what you want to do.

It's very hard to rebuild trust after someone has cheated. You have to reassess what you want from this relationship and you have to really figure out if the person you're with is a trustworthy person. Also, did you see any of this before you hooked up? I always think that's important. If you decide that, as in many marriages all over the world, it's not the most important thing to you that the other person has cheated, then you go on with it.

But I find most people don't feel that way, so you have to make a decision as to whether to stay and figure out how to rebuild your life together. Your whole life should not come apart. Yes, a section of your life has come apart. Not your life. You still have all the capacity that you had before this person cheated. What he did has messed up your coupledom. Not your life. That's how I look at it.

And you have to do it daily, minute to minute, hour to hour, half hour to half hour, day by day. That's how you rebuild. It's hard, because people are not patient. If you're patient, it's possible to do it, but you have to figure out where you're coming from with all this.

How Do You Tell Your Friend "You in Danger, Girl!" Without Being Mean About Her Relationship?

If there is a person in your friend's life who is preventing you from being in her life, that's how you can begin the conversation. You have that discussion, but you have to be honest and say something like "This person makes me uncomfortable. I just don't feel like I can hang out and be truthful, so I'm going to disappear from your life for a little while. If that's okay with you, I'm good. If it's not okay with you, let's have a deeper discussion." So maybe that will help.

There's no way to say nicely, "Your boyfriend/girlfriend is an asshole scumbag." There's no way to do it nicely except to explain, "Here's how it's affecting me." That's the only way to go at it, and sometimes you

162

have to be prepared for your friend to say, "I don't care. I'm with this person. I don't see what you see." Then you have to move on. You can't spend all that time trying to make her see what you see 'cause maybe she doesn't or can't. She might in time, but you are definitely not one of the people she's going to turn to and say, "Why didn't you tell me?"

It may cost you some time in your friend-ship. If you're ready for that, that's okay then. And if and when your friend figures out that this boyfriend is an asshole scum-bag, she will come back to you and say, "I should've listened. You were right."

CHAPTER TWELVE

First You Get the Money, Then You Get the Power

I already discussed one of the biggest issues people have in relationships, and that is sex. But just as problematic and maybe even a bigger issue is money. Talking about money can be more taboo than talking about sex. There should be no fear of talking about money in your relationship, though, and you shouldn't be lying about it, either. You should be talking about what you're doing and what your plans are together, since you're not the only one, and if you have

children together, this is even more important. They need
to be fed, clothed, housed, educated, and a million other
things. You have to remember you can't just go off and
do whatever you want, because in a relationship you have
to discuss stuff. You want a new dress, and he wants new
golf clubs, but really the kids need new school shoes. If
you buy a new dress and then he can't get his golf clubs
and the kids don't get their new shoes, there is going to
be a big problem. And vice versa.

I think the other thing—and this is a big one—one of the
other big lies in my lifetime, or in my lifestyle and experience, is that each person in a relationship contributes what
he or she can financially. It is rarely a fifty-fifty split, but
for whatever reason, when you are the woman and you
are the breadwinner, you want it to look like a fifty-fifty
split, because otherwise your man will appear to be less of
a man or will feel like less of a man. As women, we try to
bolster the man's ego. And you can't bolster your partner's
ego by contributing on their behalf to make it look to the
outside world like you're actually in an equal relationship.

What I am talking about is how we get hung up on
how things appear to other people. It was always okay
for the man to be carrying the woman financially, but
as a culture we still don't accept, or we look down upon,
the fact that a woman can also carry the man financially.

I think we should always be clear that things are what
they are. If someone's going to be with you, and you maybe

make more money than he does, you should not have to bolster his ego and buy him things or pretend he is doing better than he actually is so that other people outside think everything is fine. That's a real problem. That's something so many people do. Men and women do it, and it perpetuates bad feelings. It can perpetuate bad feelings on both sides, for the person giving away her money and for the person who is accepting the money or living off another person's money. I know only three or four people for whom that actually works, because in their case, everybody was very clear about who they were when they came into the relationship. That's why I always say that if you don't know who you are when you come in, chances are it's just not going to work as well as you'd like it to.

One thing that people forget, or go into marriage not even knowing, is that first and foremost marriage is a contract, a legal and financial agreement, and that is the way that the state and your religion, if you have one, look at it. Society sees it as your being legally bound to this person, like a business partner—except a business partner you have sex with. Too often the mythology we were raised on really affects how we go into this serious contract, giving us nothing but a bunch of romantic notions of how wonderful life is going to be. It's called mythology for a reason, people! Believe me, Prince Charming will turn into Darth Vader once you get him into divorce court.

There are a lot of people who say money is power,

sex is power. The traditional balance of power between the sexes, whether we want to admit it or not, has been trading money and sex. Things are different nowadays, where women are more frequently the top earners in a relationship, and this messes up the balance. A relationship shouldn't be about finding a balance of power, though. Sex, money, power, balance—these things exist, of course, but not when it comes to two people in a loving relationship. If you're looking for balance of power, you're screwed. You've already started down the wrong path.

One idea that should work for everyone: open a joint bank account and separate individual accounts. You should have the one account together where you're both working hard and contributing, and that's how you pay the bills: food, shelter, car, transportation, utilities, the children, and so on. Then you should have your own little money on the side for you to do whatever you want with. Once you've both agreed to this setup, you don't have to discuss it again. If you want to put a chandelier in your car, fine, and you'll avoid problems if you're buying, say, seven hundred glass elephants in various colors with their trunks raised.

Don't even ask...

Okay, you asked, so here it is. This is a true story. A woman I have known for years had a thing for glass elephants with their trunks raised, and every time she saw one she would buy it. She bought so many of them that she had to start hiding them from her husband, and by the time he found them, there were at least seven hundred. (Although, if you asked me, I would say there were about a thousand of them, but nobody would believe that, so I will go with the seven hundred.)

One day, her husband stumbled upon them in the garage, where they were hidden. He started counting them, and by the seventieth elephant, he got a little upset. He said to her, "What the fuck? Why didn't you tell me you were doing this? This is crazy. How much have you spent?" I won't tell you anymore, because then she will know whom I'm talking about. Let's just say you don't want to be that person who comes across seven hundred glass elephants in the garage, and you don't want to be the wife hiding them. It requires a lot of explaining, and that is just glass elephants.

So you need to let people know when you're spending the joint money. (Not "smoke a joint" money, but money from your joint account.) Part of it is you may actually need help if you're spending all your and your partner's money, so the other person has to know what's going on. Which is why it's better to agree to each have your own money on the side, not spend your partner's money. Besides, you don't want to have to answer to him every time you want to buy a handbag or something. You don't need to be fighting over "Why did you spend that?" Now you can answer, "Because I earned it and I have the right to spend it as I choose." And then you can buy all the glass elephants you want and not have to hide them.

P.S. This is why I live alone. I don't want to talk about anything to anyone. But if you're thinking about taking a bigger step, you should not be afraid to discuss money.

Earlier I mentioned how marriage is a contract. I am a big believer in checking in every five years with your partner on that contract, and see if you want to stay. Sit down and discuss whether you want to renew, so that you are making a conscious decision to get a new contract every five years. A lot of people think that's ridiculous, but I don't. You should ask, "Are you good? Is this still good? Is this relationship still working for you?" If it isn't working for either one of you, for whatever reason, it gives you the opportunity to discuss why and resolve the issues in a rational way. If it's not working and you don't renew the contract, part amicably so that the lawyers don't get all your money, and you can keep it to raise the kids and get on with your life without years of drama and expense and bullshit.

A book came out earlier this year called *Primates of Park Avenue*. It was fantastic. I listened to the audiobook and just loved it because it is totally clear that these women in New York City's Upper East Side entered into marriage as a business arrangement. The women treat their household, their children, their appearance, and their marriage as if they were part of a business. They don't make any money themselves, despite being extremely smart and well educated. They go to yoga and Pilates. They even get bonuses from their husbands for things like their kids getting into the right preschool.

Everybody goes into it knowing exactly what's at stake. As the wife, you have to look a certain way. If you put on some pounds, you do not receive your jewelry bonus. If you take the pounds off, then you'll get it. You'll get a bonus for having a baby, too.

Now, *Primates of Park Avenue* is about people with lots of money who are well educated, smart. I find it incredibly frightening that this is what they consider marriage.

But, see, this is the thing. It *works* for them. So I'm not judging.

If it works for you, okay. It ain't my cup of tea, though.

When someone buys you, they buy you lock, stock, and barrel. If you marry for money, be prepared to give up everything for money.

A friend of mine has a friend whose husband wanted her to augment her chest. She asked my friend what he thought. What did my friend say? That she shouldn't have to do that for a man. He also concluded that she was going to do it anyway. She wanted the money, she wanted somebody to take care of her. It was worth it to her to look like what he wanted to see in his wife.

Now, my question is: What happens when she gets older? I have never seen an eighty-year-old lady with perfectly perky plastic breasts.

It's kind of crazy, but ask yourself, "What am I willing to do for money?"

So, in some cases, money and sex and the relationship are intertwined, whether you like it or not. As with everything else, you should know going in what you're walking into, whether you're a guy or a girl. People should be up front about what they want from you. The people in *Primates of Park Avenue* are very clear. The women say, "I'm willing to do this for that." That's the exchange. And everybody is groovy because there's no lying. Do the men and the women have this conversation, or is this just the culture they live in? No, I think the conversation does happen.

The author and her husband—who did make a lot of money as a finance guy—initially made their lives together downtown. But once they moved uptown, she started to fall into the right pocketbook, the right this and the right that. It's really funny to hear her talk about the journey.

The great thing is her and her husband's relationship never changes. It doesn't shift—they are solid. They know what they are walking into, and they are walking in together.

You might think these so-called Park Avenue primates get divorced a lot, but it's the opposite. Divorce is actually very rare, unless the lifestyle becomes too stressful and somebody has a nervous breakdown. If the guy loses his job, there is no divorce, at least not from each other. Instead, they become divorced from society, and society shuns them. Any change in your status shifts you from one rung on the ladder to another.

So even though many of us wouldn't want to be one of these Park Avenue people—though, hey, maybe some of you do—my point is that it's important to have these discussions about money, how it's going to be made, how it's going to be spent, and what happens if the marriage ends. It will prevent a lot of fights, but more important, it will balance the power. In a relationship where there's a sole breadwinner, or where one person makes much more than the other, the one with the money is the one with the power, and as I said, a power struggle isn't a healthy way to be in a relationship. Being out of balance as a couple, where you either have all the power or not enough, creates a lot of resentment on both sides.

Power in a relationship is enticing, whether it's having it or getting someone who has it. Do you realize when you meet someone and he is "powerful"—*power* has many definitions, so just think about what power means to you—that you're swept up into it. Is it real? Does it take you down a road that maybe you shouldn't go down because it's a false one? People do all kinds of things for different reasons. If you're a very, very, very, very, very, very, very rich person, your money can make you powerful. If you're somebody who has a really high-powered job, that makes you powerful. If you're somebody who is a big personality, that can make you powerful. The question becomes: When do you give up yourself to another person?

It goes beyond the "It" thing. It's about self-esteem. Chances are if you're rolling with a really wealthy man, you're not there because you fell in love. Not necessarily. For some people, yes. If the wealthy person is wealthy when you meet him, though, chances are you may be suffering from *Pretty Woman* syndrome: you think this man is going to change your life. You have to look at your motivations for being with him.

I'm watching *Empire*—spoiler alert if you're catching up on the series. Naomi Campbell plays a cool woman who is dating this eighteen- or nineteen-year-old boy. I understand as a viewer that her character's intention is to get to the father, the man who really holds the power and the money and all that. She wants to wangle her way in, so she's made very clear decisions. She knows exactly what she's doing and how she's going to do it. She's being honest with herself about why she's there, and that's how you should be, too.

You know how sometimes you look over and see a really old lady or really old man with a really young person, and your mind says, "Well, she must be with him for the money" or "He's just with her for the money"? Oftentimes that's just the way it is. Sometimes folks are willing to spend the money to have exactly as much time with a person as they want to have, and then they go away when they're done.

So don't judge. Let the old people get what they need.

Let the young people get what they need, as long as nobody is getting hurt. The minute somebody gets hurt, you have an issue. If it's true to say, "I'm with you for your money," don't lie about it. Because if somebody is looking for love and you're not on the same page, it's a little shitty. (FYI, if he's 106 and you're 34, you might give him a heart attack. So be careful.)

Sometimes when you're with a very wealthy person, he will want you to do stuff to make him happy, stuff that you wouldn't otherwise do. He may want you to change your body. Sometimes he may want you to ditch your friends. Remember a while ago I talked about the line in the sand? What are you prepared to do for this type of relationship? Know where your line is.

Remember, my mother had her advice to me about relationships. When I was younger, she said, "Look, it's not that you're not attractive; you're very cute. But you can't depend on your looks. So if you want things, you have to go to work and get them. You must do this yourself because you can't depend on finding someone to do it for you. You may not ever find that somebody." She taught me that you need to know how to steer your ship because—and this is specific to women—if you get pregnant and your husband passes or your boyfriend leaves you or whatever, you have to know how to support yourself and your child. You have to know how to get up and go and do for that kid.

When a husband would leave or pass on in the 1950s, the women were like, "I don't know where the money is, and I don't know how to make money. My husband took care of everything." You can't have that today. That 1950s "ideal" was not a good one for anybody, but particularly not for women.

Here is a great time for me to say that if you want something, buy it yourself. Make your own power. Or, since we're talking about money, make your own money. In these other relationships, where you are just milking off some person, you can get all the gifts and the perks. Yes, you can get all that, but in the end, it was never really yours. Unless you buy it yourself.

You should be able to do things for yourself, no matter how big or how small. You should be able to make yourself happy. If you want to go and get a dozen roses for yourself, you should be able to go and get a dozen roses and put it them in a vase in your apartment and enjoy them. You shouldn't be waiting for somebody to send you flowers. Those are things you should be able to do yourself. If you're making money and you see a piece of jewelry you like, you should be able to go and buy it for yourself.

It's wonderful when people give you gifts, as long as you are sure there are no strings attached, and you each know where the other stands.

CHAPTER THIRTEEN

Get the F***ing Prenup

There should always be a prenuptial agreement (or prenup) in a relationship. Always.

You want to think, "Oh, we're so happy, we're going to be together forever!" No. All kinds of crazy stuff happens in life. Just because you find the person whom you're most comfortable with, whom you want to walk through life with, doesn't mean it will continue until the end of time. So in the event that there's a seismic change, get the prenup. Then you can walk away with what you walked in with, and maybe a little more. That's the way it should be. If you don't have kids, there is no reason why you guys can't say, "Hey, this is what I need, this is what you need." It doesn't matter who makes more or who makes less.

A prenup is there simply to say, "This is what I came in with, this is what I'm taking if and when I leave," and "If we have kids, if and when we get divorced, we will talk about what to do." But the bottom line is: sign the prenup.

A lot of people get bent out of shape when the idea of a prenup comes up. They think it means that you don't trust them. They think it means that you are already thinking that you are not going to make it as a couple and that you are eventually going to get divorced.

All I can say is that a prenup is not a romantic thing, it is a practical thing. If you've learned anything from this book so far, it is that the points I am trying to make here are to be realistic, to be truthful, to talk about things up front with a partner, and to not let false expectations or immature emotions get in your way and screw everything up.

In the end, a prenup is actually a positive thing. It forces you to discuss money issues up front instead of ignoring them. We've already talked about how money is such an important part of marriage, and when you don't talk about it, or ignore it, it just becomes a bigger issue.

A prenup is an act of love. It allows you to both be clear from the beginning, to discuss things and set things up properly. It creates a framework for your relationship, and then you are both in it knowing where things would end up on the back end. Also, from then on, you are staying with this person for the right reasons, not because you are afraid he is going to take all your money if it doesn't work out.

Women, in particular: if you are the breadwinner, if you are making money at all, you need to protect that money in case of divorce. It is a well-documented fact that women and children are the ones who end up financially screwed in a divorce. Their standard of living is the one that goes down. Men have always complained that "Oh, my ex got all my money in the divorce," or they become bitter about having to pay for her or the child support. That is usually in cases where the husband and wife had an agreement, spoken or unspoken, that he was going to make money and she was going to cut back on her career and take care of the children. Which, as we all know, is a job in and of itself, even though it isn't paid.

While that kind of arrangement still exists, for the most part, wives and women partners are making as much or more than their husbands or partners. Yet they aren't thinking about the future and protecting their money in case things don't work out. That's just stupid. Is it romantic? No. But neither is working two jobs to support your children and keep a roof over your head because you didn't protect your own money.

In today's world, joint custody of the children is the norm, which is as it should be (unless one of the parents is abusive). Things have changed, and the courts want to protect the children, which means that both parents share responsibility equally. It also means that you may not be getting any child support.

So sign the prenup. It's a starting point, that's all. If the two of you ever have to appear in front of a judge, it will be simpler. He says you're making more money; you can say he's making more money. Doesn't matter. Take out the prenup and say, "This is where we are. This is what we said we would do. I came in with this. He came in with that. You keep your shit, I'll keep mine. Let's take the other stuff we have together and divide it up."

What is the use of fighting over it? The only people who make money in the divorce world are the lawyers. I haven't met anyone who actually liked her divorce lawyer, whose job is to make the two of you hate each other and fight so that he can keep up his billable hours.

So give the lawyers less to do: have the conversation and sign the prenup. It's not a nasty thing. It's not preliminary to a breakup. It's just saying, "Look, we're both aware of who we were when we came in." If your old lady is making more money than you do, be happy she's with you and be happy she's smart enough to protect herself. Don't take it personally. Why would you be mad? If your ego is bruised, then get over it; you're not a complete person yet (and you should probably reread chapter 5).

Sadly, even in today's world, when the woman is the breadwinner, things can shift in a relationship. We still have those 1950s ideas about the man being the bread-winner, even though reality today does not reflect that at all. Two-thirds of mothers work. And I read recently that 40 percent of heads of household are women. More and more women are out-earning their husbands. So if you're with a guy who has these old-fashioned ideas that he should be the one making more money because that's just how it's supposed to be, well, you're in trouble.

If your partner gets canned at his job, is he going to be pissed off if you're now making the money? If you don't know that going in, it's a conversation you might want to have. Ask him, "Are you going to have an issue if for some godforsaken reason I end up making more money or I'm the breadwinner?"

Interestingly enough, this is not a conversation gay people have with each other. It's a conversation only heterosexual people have. It's the craziest thing. I figure whoever is making money and feeding the kid and keep-ing the house together, how can you bitch? If it happens that your wife is the person who is earning more money, celebrate. Celebrate that she doesn't mind and is willing to work her ass off to take care of your family. It's not a bad thing.

This is a subject I've always dealt with. I always made more money than most of the men I knew. It seems to have always been an issue, and I never understood why. "I was like this when you met me; you knew whom you were dealing with. It was part of the reason you liked me, because I was independent and I could go do things I needed to do to take care of myself."

If your manhood is tied up in your wallet, there's a problem. Men are smart enough to know that they are not defined by their penises. It's like women are not defined by their breasts or their vagina. There were women who had mastectomies and believed that their lives as women were done because they were all wrapped up in the physical as defining who they were. "These breasts make me a woman," or "Having this baby makes me a woman." None of that defines you as a woman. Just like your penis doesn't define you as a man. And your wallet doesn't define you as a man. Your person defines you as a man.

I also feel like a woman earning more than a man is something people wind the man up about. Guys wouldn't wind themselves up about it if people weren't whispering around them. A guy's family can wind him up, when they say things like "Why is she making more money? What kind of man are you?" If you're not a layabout, then you shouldn't have any problem with that kind of nonsense. If you're not a skeevy kind of person who sucks the life out of people, you shouldn't feel so bad about yourself. Contribute in other ways.

Some people are gold diggers, and that's just the way

it is. Males and females. Gay or straight. You don't want to be with those people. They come late to the party, and then they want all the money. If a couple has been married for five years and the man was previously married for twenty years, and the kids have been there since the beginning, why is the five-year wife entitled to any money? Why do you want to be with someone who thinks she is entitled like that? She's mad that she's no longer going to have the lifestyle she had when she was married to the guy. But see, she probably wasn't doing shit to ensure that she could live independently, even though she could. It really pisses me off when somebody dies, and some widow who was late to the game, who arrived late in his life, sits there and thinks she deserves all the money.

If you built a successful company over twenty-five years or busted your ass putting money in the bank or in real estate and then get married, why should that guy get your house, your car, or your cash if you get divorced?

There are plenty of entitled people out there, though, and in some ways the law protects them, unless you have a lawyer who is extremely aggressive. It is better to just say, "Hey, I spent my time, my talents, my energy creating this company and I need to protect that. It is my life's work." Or you may want to save your assets for your children or your grandchildren. So just put that down on paper and get him to agree to it. If he doesn't agree to it, then that is a red flag and you may want to reevaluate why you are marrying him.

It would make it a lot easier to figure out if you want to be with someone if the guy looked at a prenup and said, "If you leave me, I'm coming after you for money because I think that's the kind of person I'm going to turn into. So I'm not signing anything." That gives you the opportunity to say, "I don't know if I want to be with you then. Why do I want to be with someone who will want to make my life miserable if things don't work out for whatever reason?" You should have that conversation up front. It's all good to know.

If you have a prenup, you can show the time line for how shit (meaning assets) got built, making it a lot easier than going in years later without any evidence and saying, "Well, I *think* this is what happened." You don't want to do that. If you're smart, you will put a contingency in there in the event you and your partner start making a lot of money, and how you will deal with that. Put it all down on paper. It doesn't mean you like each other less or like each other more. It just means you want to be clear. "I'm helping you here, and we're doing this together. You are the front person. I'm the person in the back who is keeping all the balls in the air to make sure you're able to get what you need. So I should be entitled to a little something-something."

I also think prenups are smart because you both go

into the relationship knowing where the other person stands financially and where the other person's emotions stand with regard to money. What are his issues and what are his expectations? Lay it out. Whatever your circumstances, a prenup is reassuring. It lets you know that you and your partner are staying in the marriage for the right reasons, not because you want his money or think you will get a big payday.

How Do You Compromise with Your Spouse Without Feeling Like You Are Slowly Giving Up What You Stand For?

Somebody else asked me a variation on the same question, which is, how do you compromise with your spouse without feeling like you're slowly giving yourself up?

Look, if you're already thinking, "Oh I'm giving this up," then you're already in a shaky place. When you compromise, it is because you are both trying to figure out "how do we do this and get the optimum thing we're both looking for? "Sometimes it's a compromise, sometimes it isn't. Sometimes one person is right. But we're such boneheads as human beings that we're like, "Oh no. I'm going to be contrary just because you're not being contrary." So if you need to compromise and you have a list of things and he has a list of things, work it out to a place where you don't feel like you're giving everything up. If you feel like you're giving everything up, then you have to sit down and talk about *that* and why that is something that has come into your relationship.

CHAPTER FOURTEEN

The End of the Affair

A s happens in life, more often than not a relationship doesn't last forever. In the event that it ends, whether or not you can remain friends or at the very least go your separate ways without too many hard feelings depends on what kind of relationship you had. To me, if you can stay friends—even with someone you haven't had kids with—try to, because there was a reason you were together in the first place. You had a friendship, and people don't understand that friendships sometimes are the things that last the longest in life.

I have a lot of friends who don't understand how I can be friends with people I'm not in a romantic relationship with anymore. It's because it's not that I hate them. There was something about them I liked to begin with, I know them well and they know me well, and just because we're not romantically involved or didn't meet each other's expectations, it doesn't mean we have to hate each other.

I'm a different kind of fish, because I know when I'm done. In the past I was never able to go cleanly. I would always think, "I need to set it up so I can get out of here, and nobody will come following me." So I would let stuff linger for a couple of years before I made a move. Just because I was lazy. I knew that the relationship was over, and I was just going through the motions. So I would leave all the toys for people to play with, so I could get out of there and leave them happy with the toys.

Sometimes you have very long relationships, and then they are done. I had one for six, seven years. And then it was done. It was just done. "Gee, look at the time, got to go." It's hard to let go, but you have to move on when you get to the point where it is clear the relationship just isn't working. It isn't making either of you happy, you aren't having fun anymore, and you're not growing.

People also get hurt. They get angry. They say, "You did this to me, and that's why I left." I usually left because the relationship wasn't for me. It had nothing to do with what my partner had done. I just knew. And sometimes I get very lazy. (My friends can attest to the fact that I have let shit linger for years.) I also had other houses, so I could escape when I needed some space.

That's a huge deal for me. I need to be able to get out of town. I don't want to live with someone all the time, and at this point, not at all. I want to smell my smell in the bathroom. I don't want to be fighting the funk that somebody else has brought in. I don't think it's a bad thing. But when I'm done, I'm done.

You know the Taylor Swift song that goes, "We are never, ever, getting back together"? True, except if you're somebody I know and really care about. Things have changed, though, and now I want something different from you. I want to be your friend. I know what we were, but we're not there anymore. You have an option. You can decide to stay my friend or you can go.

So when my friends ask, "How do you maintain relationships with people after you've broken their expectations or they've broken yours?" I explain how I'm not into lashing out, saying mean things or doing bad things to someone when we break up. It happens because people are hurt and disappointed, so they're just acting out. But it isn't particularly mature. Or evolved.

I don't know how it works for other people. I only know how it works for me. There are men I will still talk to—for one, because I believe that if you've been friends or you've been lovers, you cannot maintain the anger. He was your friend, and you have to maintain some aspect of that. You don't have to see him all the time, but you have to pay respect to what you two shared. Unless he really wasn't the person you thought he was at all.

So if it isn't working, you can say, "Well, what is it?" If he says, "Well, I just can't do it anymore," you have to let him go. It's hard, but you must do it, and you can't beat yourself up for circumstances you can't change. People grow and evolve, and things change. If you're lucky, you get to do it together. In the event you don't, why be pissed? At one point you loved that person. If you had kids with him, you loved him enough to have a baby with him. So why would you want to make that person's life miserable? And are you now transferring that on to your child, and what does that do to your relationship with her? It's like rings in a pool. People don't realize the impact that bickering and fighting and shitty behavior has. (If you're a famous couple, of course, it's all over the newspapers. Then everybody is seeing it.)

Regardless, be the bigger person and walk away. If you've got to start again, you start again free, with your kid or your life. It's your decision how you are going to react. If this thing is over, wishful thinking or hammer dialing the other person isn't going to fix anything. You can drag things out, and yourself down further, or you can try to heal and move on.

This is why I'm saying that as soon as you can go, go.

As soon as you know it is not working and not going to work, be clear with the other person, because leaving someone when he doesn't know why can drive anyone crazy. Give him the respect of being clear and honest, without being mean or spiteful about it. Explain why you are going. If you don't know, you can say, "I don't know what's happened, but I know it's not going to be good for you if I stay." That is a good thing to do.

It's also a good idea to remember the time before you became sexual, because that's what fucks everything up: sex. The sex is what fucks everything up. Most of the time, I'd say you could have relationships that would last forever if sex were not involved.

Anyway, think back to that time before sex, and if you still like the idea of being friends with your ex-partner, you can say hello and hang out occasionally. It doesn't mean you're going to go to dinner, but you can be civil.

Try to do this no matter how angry you or your ex may be. People do and say things out of anger that they would never normally do or say: "You left me (or I left you), so I'm going to mess up your reputation. I'm going to make your life miserable. I'm going to turn your kids against you."

Get past the anger. It's not good for anyone.

A lot of the stuff I talk about in this book is just

common sense. A lot of people ask me, "Do you have any tips on how to get along with your ex?" I say, be polite, be thoughtful, don't let him suck you into any button-pushing drama. Don't pick a fight or discuss things that are going to make each of you angry. Just be thoughtful.

Now it does take two people to want to do it, and if your ex doesn't want to be friends or even friendly, then don't deal with him. You don't have to get along; you can just avoid one another. When you have kids, though, it's preferable that you maintain a relationship that works for everybody.

I guess the question comes down to: Is this person somebody you would have been friends with anyway? If he is, and he did an asshole-y thing, just think, "I'm not going to speak to you for a month or whatever, but I still want to be your friend once I cool off." It's easier to behave that way, rather than carry around bad feelings forever.

But if he is not somebody whom you want to keep as a friend, then maybe that's not the person you should have married in the first place, right? Why would you get into a relationship with someone you don't want to be friends with? If you don't want to be friends with him, then what is it exactly that you do want from him?

Again, it goes back to the false expectations and not knowing your own truth or what you want, and it's something you should think about if you get involved with another person.

When it comes to families, not using children against the other parent is very important. Somehow we forget that if you have children and your relationship has ended, the kids should not be used as leverage. It's so bad to do it. You will be putting your kids on some shrink's couch, trying to figure out whom to love, whom to depend on. It's very hard on children. Be big enough and handle it the right way. If you use a child against your partner, you shouldn't have gotten into a relationship, much less gotten married—you are not adult enough to know how to handle a fucked-up situation. It's dumb stuff, as bad as, say, slashing somebody's tires.

If you feel like one of the characters in *Waiting to Exhale*, you know exactly what to do. If your man is fucking around on you, honey, go and be fiercer. Cut his ass loose, because as I've said before, sometimes you just aren't the one for him and he isn't the one for you. You can get mad at him for being a cheating bastard or mad at the other woman for stealing your man, but the fact is, if things were right between the two of you, he probably wouldn't have been running around. Maybe those signs were there and you didn't really pay attention. Maybe that red flag was there and you didn't pay attention. Or maybe he's just an egomaniacal, self-centered asshole...and that's okay. You probably just shouldn't stay with him.

Let's talk a little bit about folks who find themselves in relationships with people who are in relationships with someone else. Yes, I am talking about affairs. The first thing to keep in mind is that it is quite possible that this lover of yours is not really the person you think he is. Because you have to look at the fact that he is messing around with you. Chances are he is eventually going to mess around on you, too.

I say don't be the side piece. There's nothing else to say. Don't do it, because it's not going to end well for you. It can be a dark and lonely path to go down. You will be going down that path by yourself, because no one is going to be on your side. Yes, on the rare occasion, it does work out for people, but on the whole, not so much. So if you can, just avoid it.

Occasionally your married lover will leave his wife and marry you, but remember what Oscar Wilde said, "A man who marries his mistress leaves a vacancy in that position." Chances are he's going to fill that job with someone else.

If you do marry him, you are also going to have a whole set of issues in this new relationship if he has an angry ex and kids, has to go through a divorce, and loses his sense of place in the world. He may start resenting you for messing up his life. Starting out as the side piece and ending up as the wife isn't all it's cracked up to be. You have to still be the sex goddess and confidante he fell in love with back when you were the side piece, while picking up his clothes off the floor and doing the laundry.

Beyond that, the problem with being the side piece is that the main piece hears about you and it breaks her heart. It's not your position to know what's going on in somebody's else's relationship.

Still, there is a saying that nobody can break up a good marriage. And I think that is true. I don't see why, if you had a good marriage, you would break up, though your idea of what a good marriage is and my idea of a good marriage is might be two different things.

If your married lover is complaining about his marriage no longer working, then either he and the main piece are not talking about what's not working, which is really none of your business, or he is lying to you to get some. Why would you want to be involved in that?

More often than not your lover is going through some sort of change in his main relationship—there is either a problem he needs to address or he is on his way out but not quite there yet. So you become the transition person for him. It is very rare that you're the person the man ends up with when he leaves his wife for you. I have been there; I have done that. I say this with a certain amount of authority: I have been the side piece and I have been the transition, and I am telling you, no matter how much fun it might be when it starts out, it is ultimately going to suck for you.

I also have friends who have been in both positions in this situation and found that the transition person wasn't the right one for them, but the person who came next was just right. It wasn't done deliberately, but it happened. Of course, that leaves the transition person thinking, "Wow, what is wrong with me?" There's nothing wrong with you, except that you're not the right person for that guy. You may be the right person for a period of time, you may be exactly what that person needed at that particular moment, but it doesn't mean you are the one he will be with forever. So if you can avoid putting yourself in that position, I would suggest you do so.

Just from one who has been there.

Interestingly enough, I've never had somebody say to me, "We have an open marriage, so I'm not going to be your boyfriend, but I will do a hit-and-run with you. Are you comfortable with that?" I haven't heard that, but I like it, because at least it's honest. It's better if everybody is in on the story.

But rarely do people do that, because they don't want to be judged, so they think they're better off lying. One of the Ten Commandments should be changed to, "Judge not lest ye be judged in your relationship. Don't throw stones if your house is not in order."

People choose to live in a bubble of their own creation, and some part of them doesn't want to address the problems in their relationship or they don't really want to know what their spouse is up to or thinking. It's too uncomfortable. It's easier not to pay attention. But it can be a real eye-opener when you discover that you, and everybody else around you, doesn't have this perfect thing.

So if you're not happy in your relationship, or you think your partner isn't happy, you have to look at what the causes are. If the cause is because you didn't go into the relationship honestly, it's going to be an issue. It's going to be a problem. I say that probably fifty times in this book because, to me, that basic foundation is everything.

There are people who get married when they are twenty, and they wake up one day and they are fifty with three kids going, "What the hell happened?" If you marry someone and you stay married and you wake up and it's twenty-five years later and you're going, "I never had my life," it's because you didn't *take* your life. What did you miss? Well, you raised your kids. You had the life you signed up for.

So now, if you want out because you did what you were supposed to do, that's one thing. Just say that. I think people would be more appreciative if the partner who wanted out said, "Look, we did this for thirty years and I don't want to do it anymore." That's better than slipping out and finding a side piece or turning your partner in for something younger, man or woman. Honesty is always important.

It takes us back to what I was saying earlier. The fact is a long-term relationship or marriage is not set up to be an ongoing oversexed romantic situation. That's what happens in the beginning, but after a little while, it changes.

Society bombards us with images of what love is supposed to be. The love songs, romantic movies, romance novels all give you this false sense of what a relationship is. It doesn't give you the day to day, hour to hour, minute to minute. That's what a relationship really is. It's minute to minute, day to day, hour to hour, year to year. Anyone who goes in not seeing that is setting herself up, I feel, for a fall.

In the old days, when somebody set you up—like your mom and dad would set you up in an arranged marriage—you had to learn how to figure it out minute to minute, day to day. Now people meet online and they get into a relationship and it seems great. But the everyday they can't deal with. If we spent more time focusing on the reality, as opposed to what love should be, we would have more reasonable expectations and be less disappointed. The reality is that it's not easy. It's really hard work. If you're twenty-something, maybe you shouldn't get married just yet. If you think you can handle it, try it. The reality, though, is it's not a movie.

This reminds me of another question people have asked me: "How soon is too soon to get into another relationship after you've just left one?" It's all subjective. Sometimes you could be in a long-term relationship that ends, and it was simply meant to take you down this path so you get to the person who pops up and goes, "Hey." And you know it's him. But you got to go through all your stuff.

If your gut says, "I need to spend some time with you because there's something pulling me, and there's no reason why I would be pulled if you weren't interesting to me," well, then go right ahead.

Some people try to keep themselves from doing anything too soon because they may have to heal or they are afraid that the same thing is going to happen again. They think, "No, I can't. It's too soon." You just might not be in the mood to be with another person yet. Or afraid you will get your heart broken. You know when you're ready. Not when your head tells you you're ready, but when you meet someone you like and say, "You know, I want to hang out."

What people really mean when they ask this question is how soon after you break up should you be having sex with somebody else? Well, there's always the rebound, isn't there? Or the Band-Aid or the booty call, to get you through the rough times.

Now, as I said before, looking for sex and looking for love are two different things. Sex is a thing that has nothing to do with anything. Sex is just something you do because it feels good. You can do it with anybody if you find him attractive and sexy. It doesn't require that you be in love. So, like everything else, if you are clear, and say something like "I just got out of my relationship and I'm really not looking for anything other than some good clean fun, or some good dirty fun," that's fine.

Looking for sex in a relationship is a totally different thing. You have to decide what it is you're looking to do. Are you talking about "I just broke up with this guy and I'm so devastated, I can't have sex for the next hundred years"? That's a real differentiation to me. You can go hang out with people instantaneously, and have great times with people, and develop friendships and relationships. When to start having sex again becomes a different question.

I have a friend who just got out of a relationship, and somebody came along and the two had the chemistry, but my friend fought it and fought it, but she couldn't get past the fact that they had the chemistry. It took them a minute to realize that that's what was happening. It had nothing to do with timing. It had to do with "I'm good with this. It doesn't mean forever. It doesn't mean every day. But it means 'Yeah, we can be friends. You can hang with me. We can be together.'" Once you realize that you are not messing up the last relationship when you enter a new one it makes it easier to move on. Why be loyal to a relationship that didn't work? Know that each relationship is actually different, and recognize "I got this feeling for this person and I can walk with it, even if everybody says no, it's too soon."

Besides, too soon for what? Too soon to have sex or too soon to have friends? I don't think it's ever too soon to have friends.

If you're looking for a deeper relationship that includes sex where you can bond and be together and do all that, that's a different thing. Do you want to do that right after you just got out of a long-term relationship? I don't know if that's smart because emotionally you might not be as clearheaded as you think you are. Still, you can learn how to be a friend.

One of the things that everyone seems to do when they find a new partner is they disappear. It's like "Wait, where did you go?" This is a terrible thing. It's wonderful to fall in love and go into your love cave for a little while, but you can't just disappear from the friends who have been there for you all along. That's so high school. Then, two years later, you come crying to your girlfriends, "Boo hoo, my boyfriend and I broke up!" and they don't want to hear it. They want to know "Who are you? Where have you been for two years?"

Friendships are important to us as human beings. They're the things that keep us going. We can look over and see a friend who is there to talk to and listen and watch our back and laugh with and cry with. That's who is helping you get through every day

So if you get into a relationship and make everyone else disappear from your life, I think it's very dangerous. You're then dependent on that one person, and he may not have the strength to carry all your shit along, too.

Keep some perspective. And keep your friends nearby.

How Do You Get Over a Broken Heart?

If you've read up to here in this book, you know what my answer is. You need to be a complete person with a strong sense of self and what you want, and you need to have a full life. You have your friends—which is why you don't blow off your friends the second you get into a relationship—you have your work, your kids, your passions, your causes bigger than yourself. All those things are still going to be there when the relationship is over. And although you may be heartbroken and sad, if you keep doing what you were doing, living your full life and developing yourself and continuing to learn and evolve, you're going to be fine. It will hurt for a little while, but then you move on.

And a booty call or two never hurts…

Is There Any Way to Murder My Ex-Husband and Not Go to Jail?

I hope that you're asking this with a sense of humor…If you have kids, you probably just want to murder him in your heart. You should know that murderers are easy to track down because they always make mistakes, and if you pay someone else to do it for you, it not only costs a lot of money but it will get tracked back to you.

The real question you should be asking yourself is "What do I do to quell my anger at this bonehead for doing whatever he did?" The truth of the matter is you have to make a decision. Does he still matter that much to you that his absence darkens your days and darkens your nights? Makes you unable to function in a normal way? If that's happening, you've got to go sit with somebody. Get to a therapist so you can talk it out, because the bottom line is this person

206

is stopping you from having your life. So go
talk to someone, knowing your ego is going
to be bruised and damaged. And keep going on, regardless of this idiot man you married, and eventually you'll feel better. Then,
a few weeks later, it's like, "Hey! Why have I
been wasting any time on this bonehead?"
A few months later, you'll say, "I'm so over
you!"

Now, listen. It's hard to deal with another person's anger or ongoing emotional
abuse. But the bottom line is you have to
decide that he is not worth the amount of
time you give him. That's my advice. Find
a way in your heart—I'm saying that with
BIG letters—find a way IN YOUR HEART
to master all kinds of ways to forget him.
For example, imagine putting a little kitty
cat on the stairs who will get up when your
husband is walking down, and he'll just tum-
ble down those stairs and crack his head
open. Do all that in your mind. It's like fifty
ways to leave your lover, except more interesting than hopping on the bus, Gus. Get

your friends involved, too, and soon you'll all be having a good laugh.

I had a friend who had an idea to start a new business, a website called killyourbabydaddy.com. It was a joke, but we had a really good time dreaming up that imaginary business and what we could do with it. Given how universal this situation is, we figured it would be wildly successful.

How Do You Know When It's Time to Say Good-bye and Move On?

You already know the answer to that question. When there's nothing left to talk about, there's no friendship, there's nothing there, it's probably time to go.

Now, some people, like me, don't have the cojones to absolutely cut the cord, so they let it linger for years. YEARS! It's like "I'm just too tired to do this, or maybe I'm too lazy to do it." That's really the thing. "I don't want to hurt anybody's feelings." You know what happens when you don't want to hurt anybody's feelings: you both end up hurt and bleeding and run over by a truck. Still, if that's what you're feeling, it's probably time to take that break, to make that move. Don't wait and drag it out, because it's no good for the other person and it's certainly not good or healthy for you.

How Can You Get Over Past Relationships (That Were Bad) and Not Make Your New Relationship Suffer Because of Trust Issues?

The truth of the matter is it's very hard to get over past relationships that were bad. In our minds we blame ourselves for staying as long as we did: "I stayed in this and I should have gotten out and blah, blah, blah." So each time you think about committing to a new, subsequent relationship, you think, "I should get out of this," or "Oh my god, is it going to happen again?" so you've already poisoned the well. Instead, you have to start fresh and say, "I might have been dumb about things before. But now I'm taking a new stand. This is what I'm looking for in my life."

Remember, earlier in the book, I talked about writing down the things you want in

210

a partner? Do that after a bad relationship. Don't get into the next relationship until you get at least eight of those qualities down on paper. You must make a decision about what you want in your life. Also, quit talking about what *was*. Talk about what *is* and how you will be better at seeing the red flags that you might have ignored in the past. Look and see what it was you were accepting in your old partner and all the compromises you were making. Anyway, make a list as if it's the first time and see what happens. What's the worst that could happen? It could actually work out for you.

CHAPTER FIFTEEN

Family First

Sometimes when we talk about relationships, we forget to talk about family. Our relationships to our parents, our brothers, our sisters, and our kids all inform who we are. Of course, just because they are family doesn't mean it's a relationship that's going to work—family just means you're related by blood—but sometimes there are other families that are better suited for you, more than the one you were born into.

What I mean is that the concept of family is ever evolving. My mom is gone, so I have inserted myself in my daughter's family. My friend Tom's mom is gone; she was fantastic and we both miss her, so I've inserted Tom into my family. So we evolve with the people we care about. You can't ever say, "That's not a family," or "This is not a family." It's like I said, the Cleavers are not our role model.

It starts with your parents. As you get older, you realize they're only human, like the rest of us. You want them to love you and accept you, and they drive you crazy over certain things, but you can't make them into other people. The relationship with your parents can be one of the hardest you have, but it evolves. Like, you get older and they actually seem to get younger.

Relationships with siblings are very strange, and after you're no longer living together, you ask yourself, "Is he somebody I would want to know if I weren't related to him?" If the answer is no, the answer is no. That's okay; it happens. Just make sure you're clear about why it's true, why you're tossing somebody away, or why you're withholding, or why you're jealous. You have to look at all these things.

With your siblings and your parents, you learn the importance of patience. It's a skill you must develop for all your future relationships, and you'll need it for your own kids, along with being thoughtful and kind.

Like I said, I had my daughter when I was young, and I loved her as soon as she came out. But that doesn't mean there weren't ups and downs in the relationship; it doesn't mean there weren't challenges.

My daughter got pregnant when she was just sixteen. While I wasn't thrilled about it at the time, we did have a close enough relationship that she could call me up and tell me and know I wasn't going to hit the roof. So she and her husband got married very early. And since then, they have divorced and married each other three times. That's love. It took them all this time to recognize that "It is you; you are the person I want to be with," and in order to get to that point, they had to grow up and grow apart and grow up and grow apart.

First of all, their kids were thrilled they got back together. Second, I was thrilled, because I knew that they really needed to be together. They didn't know that at first, so they had to work it out on their own, growing and evolving as individuals and continuing to come back to each other.

It took her a little while, but she got to it. So did the dad. I'm very happy for them.

So, I like my family. They are very, very nice people.

I mentioned how my mother was tough, but she taught me a tremendous amount. She understood me, she knew who I was, and she was able to advise me. My brother was also always supportive of me and helped me develop the ability to become who I became.

My daughter had her first child very young, but she's raised three insanely personable people. And now there's this new great-grandbaby who is very bizarre, but that's a whole new book. This girl knew how to work an iPad before she could talk or walk. My great-granddaughter can swipe with her little finger. It's wild.

But those relationships—you know, mothers and

daughters have weird relationships. Fathers and daughters have weird relationships. It just goes with the territory. Mothers in particular think, "I have to protect the children. I've got to keep the children happy before I make myself happy." Or "How does a man or anybody else fit into this picture of my family?"

You got kids, your first priority is your kids, period. If you're single, it might be a couple of years before you bring anybody home. As I mentioned, if you have single friends, you can arrange a hit-and-run. But realistically, those children are your life right there. Once you commit to a kid, that's your primary connection. You may have your husband or your wife, and that's great, but that child creates a whole different set of circumstances for you whether you are married or not. Other people that you bring into the picture have to figure that out, and know where they fit into the picture. You are not looking for a supplemental daddy or a fake daddy or whatever.

Meanwhile, your love life is not your kids' problem. They are just trying to be kids. They just want you to love them and they want to feel safe. If you're raising your kids, and guys are coming in and out, or women are coming in and out, it's not good for you. Forget the kids—the kids aren't going to give a shit, really. It's really about how you see you. You probably don't want an array of people coming in and out, because it makes you feel like you're unstable. Every night a different guy. It's like

"I'm not comfortable enough to go out and do this, so I have to bring them to my house. Then what is it doing to my kids, is it endangering them?" That's all your own shit, whether you're a male parent or a female parent, that's the stuff that's in your head.

So you are better off focusing on what your body and heart are telling you, which is take care of your kids. That doesn't mean you can't have a love life, it's just that the love life is not your priority. It can't come before the kids.

On the other hand, when you are dating someone who has kids, you're never going to be number one in that person's life. Not ever. I say this even though it may seem obvious, because I've seen so many people who meet somebody and say, "He has kids and isn't that great," and blah, blah, blah. They think that because a man is a father that he is more mature, more responsible, and there is something about his having kids that is a big turn-on. In the beginning, maybe. But as time goes on, they are like, "Why is he taking the family on vacation again?" "Why is he always with them?" "He does whatever his kids ask him to do," and "What about me?"

People don't realize what they are saying when they say these things. They don't realize they are saying, "Why are you not ignoring your children who don't live with you and taking care of me instead?"

But, honey, you are *never* going to be a replacement for his kids. Even if he has them only every other weekend.

Even though his ex is a bitch who tries to make his life miserable. To think otherwise is to be deeply misguided.

That's why I'm writing this book. Too often when we get involved with someone we forget common sense. If someone has children, he may love you, he may want to spend as much time with you as possible, but you're not going to be number one, because as every parent knows, even those who are still with their husband or their wife, when it comes to kids, the kids always come first. Everything else is secondary.

I just want people to have a better time in their relationships. And when it comes to parenting, one of the biggest mistakes most parents make is pretending that they weren't kids and didn't do the same exact shit as their kids are doing. Parents don't forget. They remember. There's a lot of stuff that parents do forget, that grown-ups do forget, but 90 percent of the time it's not their youth. They remember the music they were listening to. They remember what they were wearing. They remember what was considered rebellious behavior.

When it comes to relationships with your own parents, it's just a cycle. You go through certain things. Then your kids go through it. Then you deny you went through it. Then your mother says to you, "You went through this, too." You deny it again. Then they show you the proof, and everybody is happy. So be up front and don't pretend to be somebody you're not.

My God, I wore a skirt that you had to wear underwear with, especially if you had your period, because otherwise you could see the tampon string—that's how short the skirt was. So when I see these boys walking around with their pants hanging down with the cracks of their asses showing, I can't bitch at them. I hear all kinds of adults say, "Why don't these kids just pull up their pants?" but I remember you in your poufy rabbit jacket and your afro puffs and your big stacked shoes. You were out doing the same thing, and your parents were saying the exact same shit to you that you're saying to your kid.

Remember that, because it's important. You want a relationship with your kids, tell them the truth that they can take.

For example, if you were a Plaster Caster, be honest about it with your kids. When I was younger, rock-and-roll bands would go play the Fillmore East or Fillmore West, and there was this group called the Plaster Casters, who would make plaster molds of rock stars' penises. Those women are now in their sixties, seventies, maybe even eighties, and they have whole shelves at home filled with these penis molds. If you are too young to know about this, you might think I am making it up. But I'm not. This is the kind of stuff people did back then. It's not what I particularly did, but it's what was going on around me at the time.

We had sex as soon as the Pill came out, because you could have sex anywhere, and no one was going to come and get you. If you got pregnant in the old days, before the Pill and the sexual revolution, they made you disappear. One day the girl would be in school, and the next day she would be gone; she would be in the "home for wayward girls," hidden away so no one would know she was pregnant. But, baby, when that Pill hit, people were having sex with all kinds of people at all kinds of times.

So if you were having sex, figure that your kids may be interested in having sex, too. It's not this thing that doesn't happen. Denial doesn't make it go away. They are having it younger and younger, so conversations must be had.

If you were a Plaster Caster, you've got to say, "Listen, I get it. I tried to bone every rock-and-roll star I could find." I guarantee you the first thing that will happen is your kids' eyeballs will pop out, because they don't think of you as having ever been a youth. But you have to remind them that you get it, and that's why you're trying to help them. Some things they are not going to listen to, but when it comes to sex, you've got to try talking about it with your kids.

Some people take this to mean that they should be

friends with their kids. But that's not what I'm saying. Relationships between parents and children are funny. I don't know any tween or preteen who ever wanted her parents to be friends with her. Ever. That's the first bid for independence that kids exhibit. They're saying, "I'm over here with my friends. You feed me, I get that. I live here with you. But they know stuff. You don't know shit. I'm hanging with them." And that's as it should be, because that's how children learn to socialize. You can be friendly, and you can be honest and advise them, but you're not their friend. You have to be the hard-ass. It's part of the job. If you're going to have kids, you've got to be the one who says, "I don't care what Bobby's parents said; you're not doing that." You have to accept that they are not going to like it, or you. But your parents survived it, and you will, too.

And you're not going to like all their friends. You're allowed to say, "I'm not sure about this person." You're allowed to say, "I would like to know his parents." Obviously you love your children, and you may even like them and want them to like you, but you have to be the voice of wisdom and authority. So, you're allowed to say, "I want to go see where you're going." And "If you don't call me, to let me know you're still alive, you'll never see your phone again." And you're allowed to take the phone away from them. You're allowed to say, "Hey, we're all eating together; nobody has a phone at the table." But then you have to put down your phone, too. Kids learn from watching what you do. You show them how to respond to people, and you show them how to talk to and about people, by your example.

Let me leave you with this:

If you don't want to raise an asshole, don't be one.

I Complete Me

All this might be a lot to absorb, and some of it might be a little tough to swallow, but you might want to try some of the things I'm suggesting here, to see if your life works a little better. I'm not going to live forever, so I won't know if you've tried it and it worked for you, but I suspect that it will take you to the person you might be better off with, rather than to the person you're about to jump off with, whom you know isn't right for you.

I want people to have more fun in their relationships, but I also think this idea of not living your life fully because you are obsessed with getting a relationship or working on the one you're in, is a real waste of your time and energy. You get only this one life. So I say make it as full and complete and rich in experience and feeling and creativity and love as possible. Keep on developing yourself, and don't do it "in the meantime"; do it now, for you. For yourself.

Only by being fulfilled as a person are you going to avoid expecting someone else to provide all that for you. You will then have the perspective necessary to be true to yourself and say, "I'm okay if I don't want to be married" or "I don't need a relationship" or "I just want to date" or "I'm into serial monogamy" or "I mess around when I feel like it" or just have the occasional booty call, because you have all these other things going on in your life that are full of love and value and that occupy your heart and your time and are important to you. A romantic relationship is fun and can add a lot to your life, but think of it as the whipped cream on top of the sundae and not the whole sundae.

And that's all folks!

Acknowledgments

Thanks to Tommy, who heard everything...endlessly.
Thanks to Stephanie.
Thanks to Cait.
Thanks to Melissa.
And thanks to Lauren Marino.

About the Author

Whoopi Goldberg is one of a very elite group of artists who have won the Grammy, the Academy Award, the Golden Globe, the Emmy, and the Tony. Currently, she is the moderator of ABC Television Network's *The View*. Whoopi is equally well-known for her humanitarian efforts on behalf of children, the homeless, human rights, education, substance abuse, and the battle against AIDS. Among her many charitable activities, Whoopi is a Goodwill Ambassador to the United Nations.